HAMLET

Continuum Character Studies

HAMLET
CHARACTER STUDIES

MICHAEL DAVIES

continuum

Continuum

The Tower Building　　　　　80 Maiden Lane
11 York Road　　　　　　　Suite 704
London SE1 7NX　　　　　　New York NY 10038

www.continuumbooks.com

British Library Cataloguing-in-Publication Data
A catalogue record for this book is available from the British Library.

ISBN: 978-0-8264-9591-4 (hardback)
978-0-8264-9592-1 (paperback)

Typeset by Servis Filmsetting Ltd, Manchester
Printed and bound in Great Britain by
MPG Books Ltd, Bodmin, Cornwall

CONTENTS

SERIES EDITOR'S PREFACE

This series aims to promote sophisticated literary analysis through the concept of character. It demonstrates the necessity of linking character analysis to texts' themes, issues and ideas, and encourages students to embrace the complexity of literary characters and the texts in which they appear. The series thus fosters close critical reading and evidence-based discussion, as well as an engagement with historical context, and with literary criticism and theory.

The series was prompted by a general concern in literature departments about students responding to literary characters as if they were real people rather than fictional creations, and writing about them as if they were two-dimensional entities existing in an ahistorical space. Some students tend to think it is enough to observe that King Lear goes 'mad', that Frankenstein is 'ambitious', or that Vladimir and Estragon are 'tender and cruel'. Their comments are correct, but obviously limited.

Thomas Docherty, in his *Reading (Absent) Character: Towards a Theory of Characterization in Fiction*, reminds us to relate characters to ideas, but also stresses the necessity of engaging with the complexity of characters:

> If we proceed with the same theory as we apply to allegory [that a character represents one thing, such as Obstinate in Bunyan's *Pilgrim's Progress*], then we will be led to accept that Madame Bovary 'means' or 'represents' some one essence or value, however complex that essence may be. But perhaps, and more likely, she is many things, and perhaps some of them lead to her character being incoherent, lacking unity, and so on. [. . .] It is clearly wrong to say, in a critical reading, that Kurtz, for example, in Conrad's *Heart of Darkness* represents evil, or ambition, or

any other one thing, and to leave it at that; nor is Jude a representative of 'failed aspirations' in Hardy's *Jude the Obscure*; nor is Heathcliff a representation of the proletariat in Emily Brontë's *Wuthering Heights*, and so on. There may be elements of truth in some of these readings of character, but the theory which rests content with trying to discover the singular simple essence of character in this way is inadequate [. . .] (1983, p. xii)

King Lear, for example, is complex, so not easily understandable, and is perhaps 'incoherent, lacking unity'; he is fictional, so must be treated as a construct; and he does not 'mean' or 'represent' one thing. We can relate him to ideas about power, control, judgement, value, sovereignty, the public and the private, sex and sexuality, the body, nature and nurture, appearance, inheritance, socialization, patriarchy, religion, will, blindness, sanity, violence, pessimism, hope, ageing, love, death, grief – and so on.

To ignore this, and to respond to Lear as if he is a real person talking ahistorically, means we simplify both the character and the play; it means, in short, that we forget our responsibilities as literary critics. When, for example, Lear cries, 'Howl, howl, howl, howl! O, you are men of stones!' (5.2.255), it would be wrong to ignore our emotional response, to marginalize our empathy for a father carrying his dead daughter, but we must also engage with such other elements as: the meaning and repetition of 'Howl' (three howls in some editions, four in others); the uncertainty about to whom 'you are men of stones' is directed; what 'men of stones' meant to Shakespeare's audience; the various ways in which the line can be said, and the various effects produced; how what Lear says relates to certain issues in the play and introduces new ideas about being human; what literary critics have written about the line; and what literary theorists have said, or might say, about it.

When we embrace the complexity of character, when we undertake detailed, sensitive critical analysis that acknowledges historical context, and literary criticism and theory, and when we relate characters to themes, issues and ideas, the texts we study blossom, beautifully and wonderfully, and we realize that we have so much more to say about them. We are also reminded of why they are worthy of study, of why they are important, and of why they are great.

Ashley Chantler
University of Chester, UK

ACKNOWLEDGEMENTS

This book has been written with the help and support of a number of people, to whom I owe many thanks. These include my colleagues at the University of Liverpool – especially Nandini Das, Nick Davis, Bernard Beatty, Paul Baines and Marcus Walsh – as well as David Salter, at the University of Edinburgh, and Jonathon Shears at Aberystwyth University. Their wisdom proved vital at key points in the writing of this book, and our conversations about *Hamlet* (among other important things) were invaluable. Needless to say, any faults to be found here are entirely my own. I would also like to acknowledge the support of Cathy Rees, Barbara Smith and Chris Williams, for holding certain forts at certain times, enabling me to finish this book at an otherwise crucial point in the academic year. Ashley Chantler has been a stalwart Series Editor. I am grateful for his keen eye and good humour in reading a draft of this book under pressing circumstances: a true son of Bill. I would also like to express my appreciation to Colleen Coalter and Anna Sandeman at Continuum, for their editorial assistance as well as for their patience over my own delay. I owe a debt of gratitude too – for their encouragement in so many ways – to Mark and Louise Twombley. But most of all, I thank Carina Vitti, to whom in my heart's core, ay in my heart of heart, this book properly belongs.

AN OVERVIEW OF *HAMLET*

In the comedy *Eastward Ho* (written by Ben Jonson around 1604/05, in collaboration with two other dramatists, George Chapman and John Marston), we meet a character whose name is inescapably familiar to us. He appears, all of a sudden, like this:

> *Enter* HAMLET, *a footman, in haste.*
> *Ham.*   What, coachman! My lady's coach, for shame!
> Her ladyship's ready to come down. (*Exit* Coachman.)
> *Enter* POTKIN, *a tankard-bearer.*
> *Pot.*   'Sfoot, Hamlet, are you mad? Whither run you now? [. . .]
> (*Exit* HAMLET.) (3.2.5–8)

This is not our melancholy Dane but a comical rewriting of Shakespeare's Prince as a frantic footman: a servant who must ensure that the coach of his ladyship – one Gertrude, no less – is made ready in the instant. Evidently stressed by his task, footman Hamlet does not delay. He bursts onto the stage to berate the poor coachman for his tardiness, without even staying long enough to hear the gag wittily thrown after him, an allusion that no one could possibly miss: ''Sfoot, Hamlet, are you mad? Whither run you now?' Hamlet stays on the run too in *Eastward Ho*. His walk-on (or more properly run-on-and-off) part consists of entering and exiting 'in haste' twice in fewer than 30 lines, and crying 'My lady's coach!', before returning once more to announce, gasping and about to expire from his dramatic exertions: 'Your coach is coming, madam.' 'That's well said' is all he receives for his pains (3.2.41–2).

We begin with this parody of Shakespeare's most famous and, by critical tradition, most scrutinized of all dramatic characters, because it may well qualify as one of the earliest pieces of 'character criticism' ever written about *Hamlet*. As such, it offers a useful way of introducing some ideas about how we read dramatic character in *Hamlet*, and of illustrating why this can be such a complex process: a process which calls for some understanding of the history of what 'character' has come to mean in Shakespeare criticism, and which also asks us to reconsider how we think about 'character', its function and its construction, as an essential part of Shakespeare's skill – his art – as a dramatist. The aim of this introduction, is to address some of the basic facts and problems relating to the idea of 'character' in Renaissance and Shakespearean drama, establishing how it might be working in *Hamlet*, and how we might respond to it, as readers, audiences and perhaps even as actors. As the play that has generated possibly more commentary on the nature of 'character' than any other work of literature, any detailed discussion of character in *Hamlet*, and of the character that is Hamlet, demands such a preamble. Where better to start than with the earliest critical statement ever made about Shakespearean character 'on the run': footman Hamlet.

FOOTMAN HAMLET AND THE IDEA OF CHARACTER

The appearance of footman Hamlet may suggest something of the popularity of Shakespeare's *Hamlet* in its own time, as the play in which he appears – *Eastward Ho* – is peppered with other allusions to the play, from talk of coaches and hobbyhorses, to snatches of songs and lines of dialogue that early modern theatre-goers would be expected to recognize (Horwich 1971; *Hamlet* 2006a, 57–8). But there is more to footman Hamlet than topical theatrical name-dropping. Whereas we might still think of Hamlet as an example *par excellence* of fully rounded dramatic characterization (seeming to possess, quite famously, a depth or interiority, a consciousness or subjectivity, a sense of 'that within' – call it what we will), *Eastward Ho*'s footman identifies Hamlet's 'character' in very different terms. As Margreta de Grazia has argued, Shakespeare's Hamlet may have been notable to contemporaries less for the kind of individualistic traits we might typically assume him to have 'within' (a propensity to think rather than to act, for instance, and to stall action by thinking), than for a kind of ragged 'hyperactivity' that 'would have linked him', she suggests, 'more with the roustabout clown of medieval folk tradition than with the introspective consciousness acclaimed by the modern period.' As one of a number of contemporary 'spoofs [. . .] inspired by Shakespeare's play which explicitly calls for excited or violent motion from Hamlet', *Eastward Ho*'s footman and Shakespeare's Prince share more than just a name (de Grazia 2007, 8–9; Conklin, 17–20). Like his tragic twin, footman Hamlet cannot keep still either: it is Hamlet's own frenetic footmanship – chasing after ghosts and leaping around graveyards – that this footman mimics and which thus defines both characters alike.

This idea that 'Hamlet's signature action' may originally have been characterized by 'frenzied motion' rather than by 'paralyzing thought' (de Grazia 2007, 8) reminds us that what may now seem to us an essential part of Hamlet's 'character' – his thoughtfulness, his psychological fullness – may not always have been recognized as such, and that the idea of what constitutes 'character' can (as we shall see) shift quite dramatically, depending upon the contexts and traditions in which it has been considered. Footman Hamlet becomes especially important in this respect, as his significance lies not just in the way Hamlet is parodied physically in *Eastward Ho*, but in the kind of criticism it also makes, specifically about Shakespeare's style of characterization. Why Shakespeare's Hamlet seems to have been difficult to take seriously by the authors of *Eastward Ho* may have had much more to do with how 'character' was expected to function on the Renaissance stage than anything else, and with how Shakespeare's Prince of Denmark runs against such expectations.

It is easy to imagine, for instance, why Shakespeare's erratic Prince may have irritated a dramatist like Ben Jonson (co-author of *Eastward Ho*). Given that Jonson placed Classical models of poetry and drama at the centre of practically everything he wrote (in a way that Shakespeare did not: hence Jonson's double-edged praise of Shakespeare achieving greatness despite possessing 'small Latin and less Greek'), then, unsurprisingly, *consistency* became paramount for Jonson as a quality that constitutes good drama.[1] For Jonson, a play was to be structurally and logically consistent throughout, adhering to what might loosely be referred to as the Classical 'unities': the action occurring broadly within the same dramatic location, and within a realistic time-frame (perhaps even within real-time). The demand for this particular kind of consistency in dramatic representation is what subsequently lies behind Jonson's many criticisms of early modern English dramatic practices. In the 1616 'Prologue' to his comedy *Every Man In His Humour* (*c*.1598), Jonson lists a catalogue of what he regards as theatrical absurdities because they travesty neoclassical dramatic consistency: having 'three rusty swords' stand for entire armies on stage, for instance, or when a 'Chorus wafts you o'er the seas' and back again within a mere breath, or when a character appears as a child 'swaddled' in one scene and, through an implied but actually impossible passage of theatrical time, we see him 'proceed / Man' and then re-appear as a pensioner 'past threescore years' just a few scenes later (Jonson 2000, 244–6).

That such criticisms could be applied directly to Shakespearean drama (and to his history plays and later romances in particular) is no coincidence. Jonson's more explicit remarks about his fellow dramatist's shortcomings are equally infamous.[2] Yet in these terms, we can see how Hamlet and *Hamlet* could present difficulties for anyone expecting or seeking dramatic consistency of a factual or logical kind in the play. After all, it is only at the end of *Hamlet* that the Prince, a student of Wittenberg (whom we may reasonably have thought all along to be in his late teens or early 20s, perhaps), turns out to be in his early 30s. How much time has actually passed between Acts 1 and 5, we might start to wonder. Or is this a casual mistake, a sign of inconsistency, or weak dramatic construction (like the impossible seacoast of a landlocked Bohemia in *The Winter's Tale*)? (See Jonson 1985, 599, and Vickers 2003, 532.) Such dramatic loose-ends do not readily appear in Jonson's plots, though they have happily plagued students of Shakespearean 'character criticism' for generations.

Ben Jonson would no doubt have agreed with Sir Philip Sidney's similar complaint about plays that refuse to observe the desired and required consistencies of generic *decorum*. In Sidney's famous formulation, expressed in *An Apology for Poetry* (published in 1595, but probably written in the early 1580s), 'the mingling of kings and clowns' on stage, of high and low concerns as well as of stage characters, should be avoided: the mixing of tragedy and comedy 'with neither decency nor with discretion', in a way that would blur their clear generic identities, will simply not do, Sidney states. Such drama would produce neither the 'admiration and commiseration' nor the 'right sportfulness' required of tragedy and comedy respectively: when 'clowns' are thrust 'head and shoulders' to 'play a part in majestical matters', then only a degradingly 'mongrel tragic-comedy' can be 'obtained' (Sidney 2002, 112). Again, we can see instantly how *Hamlet* becomes deeply guilty of literary indecorum – of not suiting its style to its subject-matter – in these terms. In *Hamlet*, Shakespeare not only pits the wits of his clever Prince against even wittier clowns in the graveyard scene of Act 5, but he also has his heir to the Danish throne behave like a clown for a significant part of the play's action. In putting on his 'antic disposition' (1.5.170), Prince Hamlet becomes not just 'a walking generic outrage' (de Grazia 2007, 194), 'mingling kings and clowns' in his own *persona* no less; he also becomes, in neoclassical terms, radically and inappropriately inconsistent, and remains so moreover even when out of his 'antic' mode, by running after ghosts and jumping around (and possibly in-and-out of) open graves long before and after his counterfeit lunacy has been put on and off again. The problem Hamlet presents as a character in this sense is thus deceptively simple: he seems rarely to behave according to type. As a prince, a scholar, a courtier, a soldier – all words used to identify him in the play – Hamlet simply does not act as he should. To step out of 'character' in such ways is to affront dramatic consistency and generic decorum, according to the precepts of Renaissance literary theorists like Sidney and Jonson.[3] If a prince acts more like a clown and a madman than a member of a ruling household, how can we know what he really is? How could such a character, whose words and actions do not seem to match his status, role and position, conform to those watchwords of neoclassical dramatic representation: consistency and decorum?

Such considerations may start to explain just how and why Hamlet is parodied as such an unstable fellow in *Eastward Ho*. For as much as footman Hamlet's running around (like the Prince's antic tricksiness) disturbs those around him, inviting Potkin's question, ''Sfoot, Hamlet, are you mad?', the irony here is that unlike Shakespeare's hero, footman Hamlet is in fact acting entirely *in character*: a footman's job precisely is to run (before or beside a coach, for example). But we should not think that Jonson and his collaborators would go to such lengths to parody Shakespeare's Hamlet simply because, as a character, he might offend literary or social decorum. There is more at stake here than just a matter of style or taste. We should remember that for both Sidney and Jonson, the purpose of all poesy (and this would include verse as well as dramatic writing) is essentially moral and didactic. Again, according to a clear neoclassical literary heritage (and more particularly a Horatian one, after the Roman poet, Horace, upon whom Jonson modelled his own poetics and even his literary persona), all poetry and drama should work both 'to delight and teach' (Sidney 2002, 86–7). As Jonson would formulate it in the prefatory 'Epistle' to his comedy *Volpone*, '*the principal end of poesy*' is nothing less than '*to inform men in the best reason of living*' (Jonson 1999, 68–9). It is just because the poetic arts are seen as having a clear moral function that consistency in style, genre, and literary decorum (including what we might call characterization) are finally so important to the likes of Sidney and Jonson. In complaining about how the English stage commingles its kings with clowns, Sidney is not just bemoaning poor dramatic style, but the problem of confusing tragedy and comedy as morally purposive and didactically useful forms. To make light of tragedy is potentially to lose the point of the distinct moral lessons it could offer, and to lessen its power to affect audiences and effect change. Likewise, it is in terms of a literature that aims to entertain and to teach, and to teach by entertaining, that Renaissance dramatic character comes, in neoclassical terms at least, to be considered as performing a moral function more than anything else. The importance of consistency in dramatic representation, and in the presentation of dramatic character especially, perhaps becomes clearer. For if a character does not remain consistent according to the dictum expressed in Horace's *Art of Poetry* – consistent, that is, to its status, profession, age, and so keeping its 'state / Unto the last, as when he first went forth / Still to be like himself' throughout (ll. 180–2, 'Horace, Of The Art of Poetry', Jonson 1996, 354–71) – how can that character, and indeed the play in which it appears, operate in moral and didactic terms. How can it 'teach'?

The idea of 'character' having primarily a moral function, and being subordinate to the serviceable purposes of a play, may seem largely alien to modern audiences, who are more used to the idea of character as a locus of dramatic and psychological interest in its own right. Indeed, the very names of Jonson's dramatic characters may seem strangely quaint and artificial to us now, largely because they work to signal something unmistakable about their unchanging moral identities. We know that Volpone is fox-like (vulpine) in his cunning, first and foremost, because his name tells us so, just as the names of *The Alchemist*'s Face and Subtle or *Bartholomew Fair*'s

Zeal-of-the-Land Busy tell us something about these characters either as clever (though morally suspect) confidence tricksters, or as an equally dubious (because hypocritical) Puritan. We might think that such names are simply part of Jonson's satirical style. But there is more to it than that. This idea of 'moral unity' (of characters being 'individuals with unified personalities and moral natures' (Desmet 1992, 62)) indicates how character on the Renaissance stage was constructed through an ethical exchange, between both the playwright and the characters, and between those characters (and the actors playing them) and the audience. As Edward Burns and Christy Desmet have argued, ethical 'character' emerges on the Renaissance stage not simply from 'within', as a 'substance' or from an essential self that pre-existed the action or plot. Rather, 'character' is something that happens on stage, through the actions and language of a play's persons, and so emerges from 'without': 'character' is thus inscribed upon a role not just by the playwright but also by audiences, as they observe and judge the actions and the behaviour, the language used and the choices made by any character (Burns, 2–16, 18–37, 90–4; Desmet 1992, 3–9, 35–83). In the process, the audience might be expected to be inscribed – characterted in this sense – by having the play's ethical messages impressed upon them in turn by the play and its persons. For such an exchange to work, it helps if characters remain identifiably themselves: the villains should act like villains, the hypocrites should be hypocritical, kings should be regal, and clowns quite distinctly foolish. Character in this sense should be recognizable, and remain so by being consistent.

While we might reasonably wonder whether this kind of ethical characterization might have worked better in theory than in performance on the early modern stage, nevertheless it is closely related to the concurrent development of the Renaissance 'character' in a different sense: as a distinct literary genre in its own right. First appearing in Jacobean England as a particular, and evidently popular, form of prose sketch, the literary 'character' was a brief description (anywhere between a paragraph and a few pages long) that served to satirize certain 'types' of people who were recognizable according to their social, behavioural and moral characteristics or traits. A 'character' was thus a short, often comical, pen-portrait of the typical 'scholar', or of the 'rogue', or the 'soldier', the 'hypocrite', the 'melancholic', the 'excellent actor', and so on. With roots set firmly in the classical example of the Greek writer Theophrastus, the first English literary 'characters' appeared in Joseph Hall's *Characters of Vertues and Vices* (1608) and in the later series of *Characters* attributed to Sir Thomas Overbury (but actually penned by dramatists such as John Webster and Thomas Dekker: first published in 1614, and reprinted and enlarged in many subsequent editions) (Paylor, v–xxxiv; Desmet 1992, 36–8). The didactic point of the prose 'character' as a literary form, though, is clear. By presenting and analysing recognizable people according to their typical 'characters', they could be fixed and studied as a point of 'ethical enquiry', offering 'not just an amusing gallery of ethical types but regular exercise in reading human nature' (Burns, 35; Desmet 1992, 38). The Renaissance satirical 'character', like its dramatic counterpart, was valuable for the ethical and moral lessons that it could teach, and it could teach them primarily because such 'characters' were regarded as essentially unchanging. Fixed permanently by the sketch in which they are satirized, as well as by their own typical (and predictable) habits and mannerisms, these Renaissance 'characters' served moral and satirical purposes, both because they 'inhabit the present tense' and because their actions 'are infinitely repeatable' (Desmet 1992, 38). Only in this way could a 'character' make its ethical mark on its readers.

Given that Renaissance dramatists before this point did not readily refer to dramatic 'character' at all, but rather to actors 'parts' and to an actor's 'personation' of a part or role (Palfrey, 177–82; Stern, 77–90, 123–36), it is easy to see how the satirically loaded Renaissance prose 'character' would become broadly synonymous with the idea of dramatic character as something essentially fixed: identifiable, that is, by certain unchanging traits or types of behaviour (not unrelated to what Jonson might refer to as a character's 'humour': its whims and affectations as well as its 'individual pathology' (Jonson 2000, 11–18, 59)). As a preface to his later comedy *The New Inn* (first performed in 1629, and published in 1631), Jonson even goes so far as to present a description of 'The Persons of the Play', giving not just their names and roles, but detailing too their personal traits, mannerisms, and foibles: he calls this 'characterism' (Jonson 1984, 57–62). The point in drawing attention to this Renaissance sense of a fixed 'ethical character', as found on the stages of Elizabethan and Jacobean England and in the pages of printed collections of prose 'characters', is that it underlines the crucial and obvious difference that Shakespeare's Hamlet makes as a dramatic person. Quite simply, Hamlet does not work according to the neoclassical, Renaissance sense of ethical characterization. Not only is Hamlet recognizably problematic in terms of adhering to the decorum of his identity as a prince (he seems to be able to inhabit any number of roles at once: prince, comedian, play-maker, revenger, philosopher), but it is also difficult to tell whether his instability as a character is part of an overall design or not. Potkin's query to the footman of *Eastward Ho*, ''Sfoot, Hamlet, are you mad?', anticipates a line of enquiry many readers might wish to pursue about Hamlet and his 'antic disposition': when is he really 'mad', and when is he just feigning? How can we tell the difference? Such questions indicate just how *unfixed* Shakespeare's Hamlet appears to be, as a character that seems to resist any straightforward dramatic identifications or categories.

Most problematic of all, from the perspective of Renaissance ethical character construction at least, is the fact that Shakespeare's Hamlet not only flouts literary decorum but, as generations of readers and commentators again have indicated, is also notoriously difficult to pin down in terms of any clear moral or ethical identification. Unsurprisingly, the same questions resurface again and again in *Hamlet* criticism, as a sign of how the play's complexities and problems circle the ambiguities and uncertainties of Hamlet as a morally inconsistent being: why he treats Ophelia as he does in 3.1 and 3.2, for example, or why he refuses to kill Claudius when he has the chance in 3.3 (a question to which we will return in this Introduction). Is Hamlet a hero, then, or a villain? Can a madman, or a revenger for that matter, be ethically consistent? Do we read him as admirable and philosophical, heroic but flawed? Or just rash, mindless, and cruel? Even the famous question as to why Hamlet 'delays' in his revenge could be countered by an equally reasonable query over whether he delays at all. For many literary commentators and readers, this refusal to adhere to the requirements of unified ethical 'character' would prove one of the enduring strengths of *Hamlet*, and of the sheer inexhaustibility of Hamlet's character as a source of theatrical and literary interest. But for the likes of Ben Jonson, and others subsequently (including actors playing the part), such a character might present something of a problem. For what do we do with a character who does not act like a 'character'? Where do we locate the value of a part that resists, if not challenges, the very notion of moral or psychological consistency?

While the rest of this Introduction will address some of the implications these questions have long held for *Hamlet*'s readers and audiences, they indicate too the significance of *Eastward Ho*'s footman as an example not just of harmless parody but of ethical (if not satirical) 'character criticism' in action. The fact that *Eastward Ho*'s Hamlet is given to us as a footman (rather than any other kind of madcap servant) gives us a very specific clue, for instance, about how this theatrical skit works in targeting Hamlet's own flouting of Renaissance 'character' formation. When we read the witty prose 'character' of 'A Foote-man' that appears in Sir Thomas Overbury's collection of *Characters* (in the expanded edition of 1615), it seems that some early modern joke about 'character' may have been afoot all along in *Eastward Ho*. Like *Eastward Ho*, this Overburian sketch of 'A Foote-man' too makes some easy gags about his restless role as a runner: a footman's legs are said never to be alike, because he is always 'setting his best foot forward', and he 'will neuer be a staid man', so the pun goes, 'for he has a running head of his owne', and so on. But the most significant point of this particular 'character' sketch rests in its final quip about the essentially *characterless* nature of 'A Foote-man'. Unlike other Renaissance prose 'characters', the problem with a footman's 'character' is quite simple: 'Tis impossible to draw his picture to the life', we are told, '[be]cause a man must take it as he's running' (Overbury, sigs. K2v–K3). Because he is always running, no one can ever say what the character of 'A Foote-man' really is: his 'character' is impossible to 'draw' and, by implication, to see or to read, because he is never in one place long enough for it to be registered or recorded. The joke all along, then, is that the restless footman cannot be said to have any 'character' at all.

With this witticism in mind, we can see what footman Hamlet might be saying on behalf of Jonson and his neoclassically minded collaborators in *Eastward Ho*. Given not just his propensity to dash around like a madman, but also to remain radically unfixed in almost every other way, the problem with Shakespeare's Hamlet might be clear for the writers of *Eastward Ho*: he simply has no identifiable 'character'. For like the 'character' of 'A Foote-man', so it is with Shakespeare's Hamlet: it may seem 'impossible to draw his picture to the life, cause a man must take it as he's running'.

READING INCONSISTENCY

Eastward Ho's critique of Shakespeare's Hamlet as too inconsistent, and too physically and verbally wild, to function as a dramatic character ought, can certainly put into perspective some of our more recent critical debates. The arguments of those critics who regard Hamlet primarily as a non-character, as 'pure deferral and diffusion, a hollow void which offers nothing determinate to be known', may now seem much less radical or challenging in the face of footman Hamlet, who has already served to make this point well in advance of us (see Eagleton, 72; see also Barker, 22–37, and Belsey, 33–42). But *Eastward Ho*'s treatment of Hamlet as a problematic 'character' has had a long-lasting legacy in other ways. As Brian Vickers, John Lee and Margreta de Grazia (among others) have illustrated, throughout the eighteenth century – the period in which critical interest in Shakespearean 'character' became properly established – it was Hamlet's inconsistency that remained the play's chief point of interest and contention.[4] When in 1770 Francis Gentleman described Hamlet's character as a whole 'heap of inconsistency', we can see how neoclassical principles of characterization had come to dominate eighteenth-century tastes, as formulated by writers and critics such as John Dryden and Thomas Rymer (grandsons of Ben both) from the Restoration onwards (Lee, 104–9). But equally, Hamlet's inconsistency comes to be cited by Francis Gentleman and others in this period as a sign of Shakespeare's exemption from neoclassical rules, as a dramatist whose 'natural' genius lay in his ability to give us personae who appear to us, as Alexander Pope and Samuel Johnson recognized, as real individuals rather than dramatic representations: as works of Nature rather than of Art.[5]

What eighteenth-century criticism of Shakespeare bequeathed to us, though, was more than a lasting sense that Shakespeare managed to create people that seem more 'real' or life-like than those of other dramatists. Rather, eighteenth-century literary commentary shows that Hamlet (and *Hamlet*) could be defended against neoclassical charges by resorting to other criteria. Commentators sought to establish Hamlet's 'consistency' elsewhere, in fact: in his mind, psychology and inner motivations. It is from the eighteenth century onwards that Hamlet's outward inconsistency as a dramatic character came to be read against an interior consistency (of 'that within') which may be hinted at in the play, but which is otherwise hidden:

hidden from us, from other characters, even from Hamlet himself. An idea of Hamlet as consistently inconsistent thus emerges from a desire (and an ability) to explain Hamlet's sometimes baffling behaviour as something other than just poor characterization or lack of decorum. It is rooted instead in an idea of inward 'character' that, at its core, could in fact be seen as unified in psychological (and psychologically 'realistic') terms (see de Grazia 2007, 7–22).

Romantic commentators of the late eighteenth and early nineteenth centuries would make some famous claims about Hamlet's character on this basis. The German writer Johann Wolfgang von Goethe, for example, has his fictional hero Wilheim Meister declare Hamlet's 'inconsistency' unquestioningly, but he then explains it as entirely consistent with the character of a gentle and sensitive prince, a 'royal flower', who finds himself in circumstances with which his 'lovely, pure, noble and most moral nature' cannot cope. Hamlet naturally 'sinks beneath a burden which it cannot bear and must not cast away', according to Goethe, because the duty of revenge is placed upon him like 'an oak-tree planted in a costly jar, which should have borne only pleasant flowers; the roots expand, the jar is shivered'. It is this cracking-up of Hamlet that explains why, when faced with the 'impossibilities' that are 'required of him', he seems to become inert, lost in his own thoughts, and incapable of action (Bate 1992, 303–7). For Samuel Taylor Coleridge, Hamlet suffers, quite simply, from 'an overbalance in the contemplative faculty', whereby 'man becomes the creature of meditation, and loses the power of action.' All of this is, for Coleridge, 'beautifully illustrated in the inward brooding of Hamlet', in 'the lingering and vacillating delays of procrastination', all 'the effect of a superfluous activity of thought. His mind unseated from its healthy balance, is for ever occupied with the world within him' (Bate 1992, 134–5). Defining 'Hamlet's character' as 'the prevalence of the abstracting and generalizing habit over the practical', so much so that 'every incident sets him thinking' and thereby prevents him from taking action, it is easy to see why Coleridge identifies closely with Shakespeare's Prince: 'I have a smack of Hamlet myself, if I may say so' (Bate 1992, 160–1). Yet William Hazlitt would read Hamlet in just such terms: as 'a character marked by [. . .] refinement of thought and sentiment' who, 'forced from the natural bias of his disposition by the strangeness of his situation' is 'incapable of deliberate action'. Such a Hamlet is nothing less than 'the prince of philosophical speculators' (Bate 1992, 325).

It is clear to see how these readings sweep the neoclassical difficulties of Hamlet's inconsistency beneath assertions of inner, psychological consistency instead. But this in itself can lead us into some difficulties. The problem with Goethe's reading of the Prince as a sensitive flower is that it gives us a somewhat sentimentalized Hamlet, which A.C. Bradley was happy to dismantle (Bradley, 84–9), and which the play itself seems rarely to support. Likewise, Coleridge's psychological diagnosis of Hamlet as suffering from a 'disease' of the mind (Bate 1992, 157) would result in a long line of other speculative judgements about Hamlet's medical and psychological conditions, equally difficult to prove from the text alone. Sigmund Freud, for instance, takes the approach of Romantic critics like Goethe and Coleridge to an extreme, by diagnosing Hamlet's 'pathologically irresolute character' as indicative of an 'excessive development of intellect' (typical of a 'neurasthenic', he notes), and by identifying the Prince's problem as stemming ultimately from repressed and unconscious Oedipal desires (Freud, 365–8).[6] No less diagnostically, A.C. Bradley comes to terms with Hamlet's oddness as a tragic hero (upon whose 'peculiar character' the 'whole story turns') by identifying him as suffering, more modestly, from melancholy (Bradley, 73, 89–107). This condition, like Freud's Oedipal repression, provides Bradley with a key that unlocks the mystery of Hamlet once and for all, defining his character as inwardly unified and consistent with that of the Renaissance melancholic, whose mind has been 'poisoned' and 'diseased' by his condition (Bradley, 99, 101).[7]

As much as Coleridge and Hazlitt, Freud and Bradley have enriched our critical understanding and appreciation of *Hamlet* in innumerable and lasting ways, the problem presented by their readings of Hamlet's character is clear. By addressing Hamlet's 'mind' as the source of his character, whether in terms of Coleridge's over-balanced imagination or of Freud's even deeper sense of unconscious forces at work in the Prince, such critics lay themselves open to the great charge fired against so much 'character criticism' by its twentieth-century opponents: they are forced to look beyond and behind the play for evidence of a consistent, unified sense of self 'within' the character. As John Lee puts it, any attempt to establish 'the germ of the character' of Hamlet in the way proposed by Coleridge and Freud (among others) can be viewed as 'dangerous' because 'it allows the literary critic to ignore the words of the text and to produce instead a version of what the Prince "really means" ', particularly when a critic 'takes the interior of the Prince to be an unexpressed area, and proceeds to fill this gap with his own reading, which reading he then uses to control what the Prince expresses' (Lee, 132).

Attempting to fix Hamlet's character from 'within' could lead to the speculative and ultimately reductive kind of 'character criticism' refuted by L.C. Knights in his essay, 'How Many Children Had Lady Macbeth?' While Knights perhaps overstates his case in this famous (and polemical) piece, nevertheless his point is salutary: reading 'character' as if autonomous or separate from the work in which it appears, and of which it forms an organic part, can be critically misleading (Knights 1946, 1–18). Of course, inferring and speculating about characters' motivations, as A.D. Nuttall has rightly responded, will always be central (because it is natural) to the way in which we read Shakespeare's dramatic people as (to rephrase Hamlet's description at 3.2.34) 'imitations of humanity': as 'possible human beings' rather than 'just as functions in a formal system' (Nuttall 2007, 168–9).[8] But how we approach a character like Hamlet, including what we are invited reasonably and realistically to infer from his words and actions, must still be centred in our reading of the play. What we might say about the 'penumbra of inferences' that can surround any Shakespearean character, in other words, must at least be 'constrained by genuine probability' (Nuttall 2007, 176).

The formal aspects of Shakespeare's dramatic art must be given our full attention, then, if we are to go beyond the narrow limits of the kind of 'character criticism' that has long provided 'beleaguered individuals with strategies for coping' with 'apparently unmotivated actions' (Desmet 1992, 72). We should direct our critical energies, in other words, not just to what Hamlet says or does as if in isolation, but to and with whom he speaks (or jests or fights) and when: that is, under what specific dramatic circumstances (in which particular scene, and as part of what dramatic sequence overall), as well as in terms of how Hamlet's words and actions relate to matters of genre and performance, and what expectations we have of each. As Bert O. States remarks, the 'careful study of a character' requires 'full attention to everything involved in the illusion of character', including 'its duration and continuance offstage, its implied past [. . .] in a word its suggestiveness' (States, 184). To recognize such 'suggestiveness' demands in itself a deep attentiveness to the text and to the dramatic and rhetorical techniques from which 'character' emerges.

Rather than beginning with a preconceived theory about who and what Hamlet is (Goethe's 'royal flower', for example, or Coleridge's meditative man, or Freud's Oedipal prince), it may be more appropriate to read 'character' as something that unfolds through the play's action and language (and through our responses to them too), rather than as that which stands fixed somewhere behind or beyond the drama. By addressing *Hamlet* in ways that cross a number of interpretative fields simultaneously (textual and contextual, rhetorical and theatrical, generic and poetic), such reading can begin to show us that a character like Hamlet cannot be reduced easily to any consistency. As with *Eastward Ho*'s footman, it can be difficult simply keeping up with a character formed like this.

RE-READING DELAY

To illustrate how *Hamlet* places clear and exacting demands upon us, and to ensure that we are reading the Hamlet within *Hamlet* rather than one without or beyond the play, let us turn briefly to a scene notorious for its openness to contradictory readings of Hamlet's character: 3.3, in which Hamlet, hot-footing it to an interview with his mother, the Queen, comes across the King, his uncle, at prayer. In the most recent Arden edition (*Hamlet* 2006a),[9] based on the Second Quarto of the play (first printed in 1604/05), this is what Hamlet says in soliloquy (the King, though also on stage, cannot hear him):

> Now might I do it. But now 'a is a-praying.
> And now I'll do it [*Draws sword.*] – and so 'a goes to heaven
> And so am I revenged! That would be scanned:
> A villain kills my father, and for that
> I, his sole son, do this same villain send
> To heaven.
> Why, this is base and silly, not revenge.
> 'A took my father grossly and full of bread
> With all his crimes broad blown, as flush as May,
> And how his audit stands who knows, save heaven,
> But in our circumstance and course of thought
> 'Tis heavy with him. And am I then revenged
> To take him in the purging of his soul
> When he is fit and seasoned for his passage?

No. [*Sheathes sword.*]
Up sword, and know thou a more horrid hent
When he is drunk, asleep or in his rage,
Or in th'incestuous pleasure of his bed,
At game a-swearing, or about some act
That has no relish of salvation in't.
Then trip him that his heels may kick at heaven
And that his soul may be as damned and black
As hell whereto it goes. My mother stays;
This physic but prolongs thy sickly days.

(3.3.73–96)

Putting aside the 'red herring' of plot continuation (the idea that Shakespeare must somehow avoid Hamlet actually killing Claudius in order to keep the story going), Hamlet's decision not to exact his revenge here pushes us into some tricky terrain when it comes to reading his character. Hamlet's sentiments – his desire not just to kill his uncle, but to sentence him to eternal perdition, to send his soul 'damned and black' to hell – are unequivocally awful. No wonder Samuel Johnson could not bear this speech, 'in which Hamlet, *represented as a virtuous character*, is not content with taking blood for blood, but contrives damnation for the man he would punish': this is, Johnson notes, 'too horrible to be read or to be uttered.' (Johnson, 242, emphasis added). No wonder too, as de Grazia reminds us, that this speech would be omitted from many productions in the eighteenth and nineteenth centuries, for being just too offensive to dramatize: offensive not just to tender religious sensibilities, but also to the idea of Hamlet as a tragic hero, the 'virtuous character' with whom we might be expected to identify ethically and morally, and who should, we might think, invite our sympathy and pity (de Grazia 2007, 158–60).

Such horror and upset would be entirely unnecessary, though, if we could say that Hamlet does not really mean any of this, which is precisely what other commentators of the late eighteenth and early nineteenth centuries went on to suggest. William Hazlitt argues, for example, that the 'malice' Hamlet expresses at this point is meaningless because 'in truth' it is 'only an excuse for his own want of resolution' (Bate 1992, 325): a rhetorical smokescreen behind which Hamlet can safely defer the murderous deed of which he is, by nature, characteristically incapable. For Hazlitt, this decision (or is it really an indecision?) is a reflection of Hamlet's true 'character', the chief characteristic of which is to delay, speculate and philosophize. For Coleridge this is so manifestly the case that he even takes baffled offence at Dr Johnson's insensitivity in misreading this speech so grossly: for 'mistaking' the speech's clear 'marks of reluctance and procrastination' (Hamlet's characteristic propensity to delay and defer action again) for signs of 'impetuous, horror-striking, fiendishness! – Of such importance is to understand the germ of a character', Coleridge triumphantly concludes (Bate 1992, 320).

So what do we do? Is Hamlet being demonic in 3.3, or just weak, or even cowardly? Fiendish, or just sensitive and philosophical? It seems that the only way to reconcile the damnable speech of 3.3 with any notion of Hamlet's character as 'virtuous' is either to excise it from the play completely (as Johnson censoriously desires, and as the eighteenth-century actor-manager David Garrick put into practice), or to assume (with Hazlitt and Coleridge) that Hamlet does not actually mean what he says in the speech, and (unknown even to himself, perhaps) that he is really finding a convenient excuse to avoid doing what he has to do, so that he can do instead what he always does: think, procrastinate, and delay. To a certain degree, the speech itself can support such a reading, given that Hamlet's initial strengthening in resolve (from 'Now might I do it' to 'now I'll do it') seems to dissolve just as quickly into deeper theorizing. Hamlet's words also appear to mimic thought processes, as they move through some metrically unstable lines of verse, barely held together by the Second Quarto's looser punctuation, while circling the keyword 'revenge' repeatedly (ll. 75, 79, 84). The most finely balanced line (l. 83, which, like a rhetorical hinge, stands right at the centre of this soliloquy) confirms the place of contemplation at the heart of this speech by describing it exactly: Hamlet weighs the 'audit' of his father's fate and his uncle's 'crimes' against one another 'in our circumstance and course of thought' (ll. 81–4). As with so many of Hamlet's speeches and soliloquies, such words give us a characteristic impression of 'thought' happening before our very ears. It is in the drama of such thinking, presumably, that Coleridge might find evidence for the 'germ' of Hamlet as a contemplative man, as an over-thinker rather than an over-reacher.

But does this speech exemplify any such characteristic delay, as has so often been presumed? Perhaps not. Hazlitt and Coleridge might wish to rescue Hamlet from charges of fiendishness, but they do so by reading an idea of Hamlet's hidden character onto the soliloquy, having already fixed it beforehand, rather than seeing it as something that arises from the text. The fact that Hamlet stops to think so carefully about his situation at this point might serve to signal Hamlet's frightening *decisiveness* more than anything else. After all, Hamlet's decision not to kill Claudius comes not through any delicate or sensitive musing here, but via a carefully developed line of reasoning, both sharp and clear, in a way that makes this speech's 'course of thought' no abstract philosophizing but a sure process of vengeful calculation. Like some sinister accountant, Hamlet hesitates not out of doubt or uncertainty here, but merely to 'audit' better Claudius's future fate against the remembrance of his father's murder, taken 'full of bread / With all his crimes broad blown' (ll. 80–1). There is, perhaps, nothing more decisive or more lucid in the whole play than the fearful reckoning Hamlet makes at this point, and which concludes in the singular 'No' that he utters at l. 87, which stuns the unsteady metrical patterns of the verse through the sharpest of hypometric lines (of just one syllable), and which freezes the action before moving the speech into a final confirmation of hotter, more hellish plans, delivered to us now in lines that become metrically more consistent, more secure, more resolved. Hamlet's singular 'No' shifts this soliloquy into a cooler regularity that communicates the heat of black desires even more intensely. He has, in other words, made up his mind very firmly indeed.

Hamlet is far from lost in thought in this scene, and far from uninterested in taking action. He is, rather, more deeply committed to exacting a far more profound and sinister kind of revenge than we might have previously imagined. While his pause here may be reminiscent of the avenging Pyrrhus, whose horrid hesitation before slaying the aged Priam is recounted by the player before Hamlet in the 'Hecuba' speech of 2.2.406–35, Hamlet's strategic postponement in 3.3 is compatible neither with the Romantics' sensitive philosophical prince, the 'royal flower' of Denmark, nor with Johnson's 'virtuous character'. But it is consistent with the character of a Renaissance revenge hero: the kind of stage-avenger whose role Hamlet accepts from the Ghost in 1.5 (and whose words he echoes quite clearly in the soliloquy of 3.3), and into the 'character' of which he steps most fully at the close of 3.2 (the last time we will have seen Hamlet on stage, in fact). Having proof at last (as he sees it, at least) of Claudius's guilt, Hamlet exits 3.2, we should recall, vowing how in 'the very witching time of night / When churchyards yawn and hell itself breaks out' he will be ready to 'drink hot blood' and 'do such business as the bitter day / Would quake to look on' (3.2.378–89). So, having become at last the revenge hero we have been waiting for him to become – 'the real stuff', as one commentator has described it (Mercer, 213) – Hamlet unsurprisingly voices no ethical objection to killing the defenceless Claudius while at prayer, and expresses no pangs of conscience about his task overall. What overtakes him instead is a profound bitterness at the idea of sending his father's murderer to heaven 'in the purging of his soul' (3.3.85). How would this be 'revenge'? For as the Senecan dictum has it, '*scelera non ulcisceris, / nisi vincis*': crimes are not avenged, unless they are out-done or exceeded.[10] An eye for an eye, a life for a life will not do, in other words: the revenge taken must be more horrid than the wrong originally committed. As an avenger, then, Hamlet's noble contempt towards such scant revenge is duly scanned in the 1604/05 Second Quarto's speech: to kill Claudius at prayer is not just 'hire and salary', as the Folio version of 1623 has it, but even more ignobly, and plainly, it is 'base and silly' (3.3.79).

The full irony of Hamlet's situation in 3.3 thus becomes clear. Only by postponing murder in the name of revenge – only by refusing to kill Claudius at prayer – can Hamlet become a proper revenge hero. As Peter Mercer has argued, delay is simply the name of the game when it comes to revenge. It gives the avenging hero-villain time to develop his devious plans in what is always 'a business of cunning plots and secret devices of death', but which also calls for 'the revenger to strip himself of every vestige of nature' in the process (Mercer, 3, 6). The effect of Hamlet's cold hatred, of damnable thoughts that threaten to send his own soul to hell as certainly as his victim's, is finally so awful because it reveals how far Hamlet, as a revenger, is prepared 'to destroy his own humanity'. This is the traditional fate of the revenger: to become himself a 'spectacle of loss' (Mercer, 5, 6). Such is Hamlet's fate in 3.3, made with brilliant dramatic force by Shakespeare, who takes full advantage of the dramatic irony involved: Hamlet can only assume the identity of revenge hero, both truly and fully, by *not* killing Claudius in 3.3, thereby becoming at this moment something more than just a seeker of rigid justice or a rash, impetuous killer (which is what he becomes in the next scene, of course, in killing Polonius). As a revenger, the Hamlet of 3.3 becomes something colder and more monstrous, yet at the same time all too human, or rather all too humanly inhuman. No wonder Johnson was terrified.

As horrifying as the 'pure diabolism' (de Grazia 2007, 191) of this avenging monster might be, reading Hamlet's speech of 3.3 within the generic frame of revenge tragedy at least allows us to grapple with the character that we find in the play. Why would Hamlet the avenger not mean just what he says here? How can we take him at anything other than his word? But equally we might also wonder whether this is the Hamlet that *Hamlet* really gives us in 3.3. As we would expect, there is more to it. What complicates our response to Hamlet's speech and his transformation, as a 'character', into a diabolical revenger might have less to do with questions of 'inward' or 'psychological' character and unconscious motivations than with the way in which Shakespeare has structured 3.3 according to a dramatic irony that requires us to adjust our view of 'character' continuously. Most obviously, the fact that Hamlet does not stay long enough to hear the final lines of the scene – in which Claudius admits that he cannot repent (3.3.97–8) – changes our view of Hamlet's damnable speech instantly. Our knowledge that Claudius has not repented after all somehow punctures Hamlet's awful reasoning about revenge the very instant he leaves the stage, by revealing it to have been pointless all along. If only Hamlet had not been in such a hurry, if only he had been *less* decisive and paused for *longer*, we might think, then this could have been a great opportunity to fulfil his task. But we can only see this by reading to the end of the scene. Such dramatic irony cannot lessen the impact or the intensity of Hamlet's demonic desires as he utters them. Rather, it deflates them retrospectively, when Hamlet has exited, with the irony of Claudius's admission cancelling Hamlet's speech, placing it under erasure, through the disclosure of an equally grave truth and an even more consequential turning point in character: the revelation of Claudius's desire yet inability to repent of his crime, which he confesses fully for the first and only time in this scene (despite being given a taste of his smarting conscience earlier: 3.1.49–53).

What trips up our initial response to Hamlet's terrifying speech in 3.3, then, has little to do with anything that Hamlet does or says, but with what Shakespeare has another character do and say before and after we hear it. What really undermines the fixing of Hamlet's character as a stage-revenger here is not just what Claudius reveals at the end of 3.3, but what we witness him doing and saying before Hamlet arrives. As Peter Mercer has pointed out, the greatest dramatic irony of the repentance scene lies not in the fact that Hamlet could have both killed and damned Claudius all along, but that at the very point at which Hamlet seems at last to have become a Renaissance revenge hero, ready to drink hot blood, send souls to hell and all the rest, just as suddenly Shakespeare reconfigures our expectations of 'character' by presenting Claudius to us as a man who seems no longer to deserve such vengeance, or even the title of villain (Mercer, 214–16). By becoming all of a sudden a being of conscience and doubt, of racked thoughts and fearful guilt in his own soliloquy of 3.3.36–72, Claudius's appearance as something other than a heartless murderer and a tyrant steals from Hamlet (and from the audience) this supreme opportunity of revenge. Not only does it become impossible for Hamlet to murder Claudius at this point (because clearly revenge cannot work in circumstances where the villain suffers and repents), but also it is Hamlet – just as unexpectedly – who appears to have become the two-dimensional villain now, a caricatured stage-revenger, and Claudius who becomes more fully a figure of depth, complexity, and dividedness, as he speaks in soliloquy of delay and procrastination, and wrestles with repentance 'like a man to double business bound' yet left to 'stand in pause where I shall first begin (ll. 41–2). Claudius thus becomes startlingly more like Hamlet than we were expecting.

The simple yet brilliant point of 3.3 is to turn our expectations of 'character' on its head through a carefully balanced juxtaposition of ironic reversals. For a moment in this scene, it is the King who becomes the sympathetic victim and the Prince who becomes the villain, making what has been taken so often as a sign of 'character' (Hamlet's delay, his procrastination, his thinking) more of a clever inversion of revenge tragedy's roles and actions. The figure of the praying murderer in 3.3, in other words, overturns ideas of how characters ought conventionally to behave in revenge tragedy, and undermines our view of Hamlet at the very moment when he appears to have become most fully himself a dramatic type: the stage-revenger. The point of 3.3 is not that Hamlet delays because of anything in his psychological 'character', but because his 'role' as a revenge hero suddenly becomes complicated for us by the dramatic situation in which he finds himself. For as Mercer puts it: 'If there are no monsters, there can be no revenge' (215).

CHARACTER AS PROCESS

What even this sketchy exploration of 3.3 suggests is that 'character' in Shakespearean drama is not something that can be read as separate from the action of the play or from the other parts with which it interacts, or from matters of dramatic genre and audience expectation. We can see in 3.3, for instance, that what determines our responses to Hamlet's 'character' (what constitutes his 'character' at this point, in fact) is not just what he says and does in a speech to be read in isolation (always a temptation, perhaps, with a soliloquy), but how those words and actions appear in the light of *another* character's identity, and as part of an overall dramatic sequence. Given Shakespeare's masterful command of dramatic irony and scenic structuring in 3.3, we can see that 'character' emerges from the careful balancing of the parts of Claudius and Hamlet together, and not simply or ineffably from 'that within' the Prince alone. To read 'character' in this sense requires us to be sensitive to what Shakespeare as a dramatist and theatre-poet is doing on many inseparable levels simultaneously. Reading character involves nothing less than reading (and re-reading) the play as carefully and as attentively as possible: it invites and involves an inexhaustible engagement with Shakespeare's dramatic practices.

But what 3.3 also indicates is that Shakespearean dramatic character is rarely ever fixed or static. Rather than emerging from set traits and characteristic modes of behaviour associated with 'types' (in the sense discussed earlier), Hamlet resists easy categorization as a 'type' or 'character', as he is formed on the move in *Hamlet*, unfolding through the play's sequence of actions and words, and often in unexpected and surprising ways. Rather than being something that we might think of as *essential* or *substantive*, as set and unchanging from the beginning, the way that 'character' both shifts and requires shifting responses in a scene like 3.3 makes it *conditional* more than anything else: conditional less upon what we think Hamlet (or Claudius) is *in advance* or *in essence* as a 'character' than upon what happens at any given moment. A continual process of adjustment and realignment is required when reading Shakespearean 'character' as something revealed in stages, and which can seem more contradictory than coherent at times, but which accumulates depth and fullness as part of an entire dramatic structure.

Critics have recognized this style of character formation in different ways. Bert O. States, for example, who argues against the notion of discontinuity in Shakespearean characterization, nevertheless sees that a character such as Hamlet is constructed on a 'transformational' rather than a 'dispositional' basis: that is, our understanding of his character develops sequentially, rather than as something defined by a set of traits or inherent dispositional attitudes, in the way that Jonson's characters, for example, are set according to their satirized 'humours' (States, 40–1). Equally, by identifying dramatic character as what it *does* and *says* rather than something that it inherently *is*, Edward Burns and Christy Desmet have illustrated how 'character' is formed primarily through the language and rhetoric employed by Shakespeare. Reading character as a rhetorical phenomenon, determined by what it says and does before our eyes and ears, allows judgements about character to emerge on a transactional basis, arising from the audience's engagement with a part rather from anything permanently 'within' or behind it, while also making character inseparable from the immediacy of the drama as it happens. As Desmet puts it, because the 'self' of a character like Hamlet 'is a construct, a sequential representation of potential roles rather than a given, it can be spoken into existence' (Desmet 1992, 75). Each time a character speaks, it might create or reveal itself afresh, as something different from yet connected to our idea of what that character has so far become. Michael Goldman has described this effect as the result of the 'multiple movements' involved in the acting and watching and reading of a play, a process in which we see a character not just as a self made on the stage or on the page, or even a self in the making: rather 'the self *is* the making' in Shakespearean drama, because a 'character' like Hamlet is never anything more or less than what it is doing and saying (and what an actor or a reader is doing with it) 'now and now and now' (Goldman, 9–10).

This 'processional' nature of Shakespearean character, moving moment-to-moment through the play, was certainly recognized by William Hazlitt in the early nineteenth century. Although Hazlitt nailed Hamlet's character as 'prince of philosophical speculators', this identification does not preclude him from seeing that Shakespeare's characters function sequentially through the dramas in which they appear. As John Lee puts it, summarizing Hazlitt's view of Shakespearean character as a continual movement through states of 'decomposition' and 'composition', we can see how the character of Hamlet is, on a 'processional' basis, 'forever breaking and reconstituting himself' throughout the play (Lee, 142–3). As a result, the idea of 'knowing' a character like Hamlet becomes simply irrelevant, in part because 'the Prince's actions or words are not reducible to a meaning, but rather are the meaning', but also because this moment-to-moment formation resists reduction to any overarching theory that seeks to define and limit Hamlet's character according to its supposedly 'true nature'. Because the processional character of Hamlet must 'be watched and attended to' moment by moment, his words and actions can no longer be 'discounted' by the critic who believes he or she is in 'possession of his ideal principle', or the true 'germ of his character' (Lee, 139, 144).

One of the prime advantages of recognizing this sequential construction of character is that it allows us to turn to *Hamlet* as the source for understanding Hamlet, rather than anything beyond the play, no matter what might be inferred from it in terms of hidden motivations. Indeed, the business of sifting through the 'penumbra of inferences' that surround a character like Hamlet becomes part of the unfolding of Hamlet's character in sequence: it is central to our experience of reading character in process, and to our sense of how character is being continually 'filled out' by Shakespeare (Palfrey, 191). Reading dramatic character as a process (moving, shifting, changing) rather than as the product (fixed and defined) of drama offers a way for us to avoid some of the interpretative restrictions that come with assuming that consistency must be the central criterion in constructing character. Seeing character as progressive rather than essential and substantive does not mean, of course, that we cannot trace any continuity or coherence in a character like Hamlet. Yet such consistency, what Alan Sinfield refers to as a 'continuous consciousness' (Sinfield 1992, 65), nevertheless arises from the moment-to-moment revelation of character, rather than from an assumed essence existing elsewhere, outside what we can see and hear. It has little to do, in other words, with the kinds of 'consistency' we might expect from a character in a novel, or from a play in which a character can be explained through particular psychological insights into their backgrounds and personalities. Hamlet's character does not happen in the past, though it has an important relationship to the past and its remembrance. Rather, his character is what happens in front of us, at the time that we read or watch or hear it happening.

CHARACTER ON THE RUN

Because character can be read as immediate and momentary, liable to appear different in different scenes, and so might seem more discontinuous than consistent, more dramatically dynamic than psychologically determined, it also offers us other avenues of enquiry. For example, Charles Lamb, writing in the early nineteenth century, would always find *Hamlet* performed on stage a disappointing experience, because for him it would be impossible for any actor playing the part of the Prince to encompass Hamlet's inexhaustible variety, complexity and subtlety. For Lamb, the character of Hamlet could only be reduced by an actor to something fixed and inflexible, mundane and 'vulgar', leaving him to conclude that 'the pleasure which we take in seeing one of these [i.e. Shakespeare's] fine plays acted' is nothing 'compared with that quiet delight which we find in the reading of it' (Bate 1992, 111–27). Yet Jonathan Holmes has demonstrated how actors themselves have often found Shakespearean character to work against 'consistency' in just this way, resisting explanation as a psychologically determined, unified 'personality'. Contemporary players of Shakespeare often attest that his characters are rarely susceptible to singular and fixed modes of behaviour, operating instead 'from moment to moment' and with 'little psychological progression discernible' (Holmes, 21). As a result, actors such as Michael Pennington, Gregory Doran and David Tennant have often been forced when playing Shakespeare's parts 'to stop striving for the logical through-line' of a character, and instead 'to play each moment as it arrives' (Holmes, 25; see also Pennington, and the accounts compiled in Mills).

Preparing to play a Shakespearean character as psychologically real, explicable and consistent in the sense of twentieth-century Stanislavskian or Method acting can prove difficult, therefore (Burns, 1–17, 120–73). As another Shakespearean player, Ian McDiarmid, puts it: this is 'not really what acting is about' when it comes to Shakespeare, because 'the central dynamic is to be found in the collision of contradictions', between a character's actions and words, and between the play's scenic shifts and juxtapositions (Holmes, 50). As Holmes summarizes, dramatic 'identity' is 'reconfigured' by Shakespeare in order to accommodate the demands of 'extreme situations' through which 'supposedly continuous character is subordinated to the function of the role at that moment'. For an actor, then, 'to play the moment absolutely' can result in something much more holistic when it comes to thinking about 'character': it demands 'defining the role, rather than the character' both as each moment finds it, and 'in relation to the people – cast, audience – with whom [the actor] must interact' (Holmes, 50–1)

Such accounts are fascinating because they indicate how processional 'character' works from the professional player's point of view, while signalling how ideas of consistency (whether neoclassical or psychological) rarely provide the key to unlock Shakespeare's characters, for actors or readers or audiences. But reading Shakespearean character as conditional and sequential also seems apt given the textual issues surrounding *Hamlet* as an early modern play. It becomes difficult to assert any neoclassical or psychological ideas of unitary character, or to assume too confidently that we are reading the Hamlet that *Hamlet* gives us, when there are in fact three different early printed versions of the play (the First Quarto of 1603, the Second Quarto of 1604/05 and the Folio text of 1623), each of which varies from the other in a number of significant ways, and which – as we shall see throughout this book – can have important implications for how we read characters like Hamlet, Claudius and Gertrude. Can the Prince of the 1604/05 Quarto text of *Hamlet* be exactly the same as – or 'consistent' with – the Hamlet of the 1623 Folio, given that they evince different speech mannerisms in certain places? The Folio Hamlet has a habit of repeating himself, for instance, which the Second Quarto's Hamlet does not possess. They use different words and phrases at times ('hire and salary' versus 'base and silly' in 3.3, for example), while their speeches are also punctuated differently. They sometimes give entirely different speeches from one another (such as the soliloquy of 4.4, which appears only in the Second Quarto text of *Hamlet*, and not at all in the Folio text).[11] Does the description of Gertrude as 'Queen' in one speech prefix but as 'Gertrude' (or rather 'Gertrard') in another, among these early printed versions, signal a shift in her 'character' in different scenes? Does it make a difference to how we perceive Claudius that in none of the first printed texts of *Hamlet* is he referred to as such by name, his part always being preceded by the speech prefix 'King'?[12]

Such questions, and the textual issues that surround them, signal how 'character' is contingent not just upon what happens in *Hamlet*, but what happens to *Hamlet* in a more material sense: that is, in terms of what editors and directors do both to and with a play which is often on the move textually and theatrically, and which has always been cut and pasted, on the stage and on the page, to suit the tastes of its audiences and readers, whether in eighteenth-century theatres or twentieth-century cinemas. What Hamlet's 'character' is can depend as much on the decisions made by a scholarly editor or a screenwriter or a theatre director when preparing to present it to their various kinds of readers and audiences. The complexity of what 'character' means in such contexts can be dizzying. How can we keep up with a character so moveable, so changeable, and open to contradiction on so many levels? Is the 'true' Hamlet that of the Second Quarto or the Folio? Or that of editors who conflate these two versions of the play? Or of Olivier's or Zeffirelli's films? Or of John Gielgud's or David Garrick's, or Richard Burbage's or Richard Burton's, or Kenneth Branagh's or Michael Pennington's stage performances?

Issues of 'authenticity' stand at the heart of such questions. What and where the true Hamlet and the authentic *Hamlet* is – on the stage or on the page, and on whose stages or pages or screens – can be complex questions to address and to unfold (see especially Orgel 2002). Yet they also underscore something important about how we are required to read character in a work such as *Hamlet*: that is, as Hélène Cixous puts it, as something quite removed from the restrictive practices of interpretation, 'where everything is coded in advance', and quite different from the kind of reading which turns 'character' into little more an 'I.D. card', by fixing identity and repressing the more expansive potential of its 'subjectivity'. For this reason, 'character' is an ideologically sullied term for Cixous, suggesting something 'to be *figured out*, understood, read [. . .] presented, offered up to interpretation, with the prospect of a traditional reading that seeks its satisfaction at the level of a potential identification' (Cixous, 384–5). For Cixous, the word 'character' represses the very idea of a complex, multifarious self, stamping subjectivity into a 'certificate of conformity' (Cixous, 386). For her, it becomes – rather like *Eastward Ho*'s footman, in fact – 'the servant of a certain order that parades itself across the theater of writing' (Cixous, 385). This idea of 'character' can be redefined away from the fixed and knowable towards an idea of the 'self' that can be 'multiplied [. . .] into a trans-subjective effervescence', and thus aligned with Michel de Montaigne's Renaissance idea of the self as radically giddy, staggering, both inconstant and 'in constant motion'.[13] Hamlet might not be a 'character' at all, then, in the typical sense, if we see him as given up 'to the complexity of his subjectivity, to his multiplicity, to his off-center position, to his permanent escapade' (Cixous, 384). His form of characterization gives us the 'true subject' as an 'I' who is 'always on the run', resisting subjection to a fixed identity, and becoming 'that which escapes and leads somewhere else', beyond the 'treadmill of reproduction' that the term 'character' typically exemplifies (Cixous, 387–8).

We might see *Hamlet* as Cixous's *'imperishable* text' *par excellence*, recognizable as such 'by its ability to evade the prevailing attempts at reappropriating meaning' through any notion of 'character' as 'a whole subject [. . .] conscious, knowable' (Cixous, 384–5). But in this we might be reminded again of *Eastward Ho*'s footman Hamlet, as a parody of a characterless character, and yet whose appearance – with more prescience than its authors would have realized – also signals the subversive and inexhaustible nature of Shakespeare's Hamlet as a figure who seems able to step continually beyond his limits as a 'character': as an 'I' in a state of 'permanent escapade', 'always on the run'. It is not just that *Hamlet* requires us to think of character as a subjectivity that cannot be reduced to the facts printed on an 'I.D. card', or that should conform to neoclassical principles of consistency, or provide psychological coherence. Rather, *Hamlet* instructs us in these affairs. *Hamlet* teaches us to think of character as something 'on the run', and it delights us in doing so.

NOTE ON THE EDITION USED

Unless otherwise indicated, the edition of the play cited throughout this book is the Arden Shakespeare *Hamlet* (2006), edited by Ann Thompson and Neil Taylor. This edition is based on the Second Quarto text of *Hamlet*, first published in 1604/05, but it includes in an appendix (465–73) those passages found only in the Folio text of 1623. This edition is indicated in the Bibliography (and elsewhere) as *Hamlet* 2006a, to distinguish it from the companion Arden Shakespeare edition of *Hamlet: The Texts of 1603 and 1623* (2006), also edited by Thompson and Taylor, and indicated subsequently as *Hamlet* 2006b. The nature of the textual differences between the three early printed versions of the play – that of the First Quarto (1603), of the Second Quarto (1604/05), and of the First Folio

(1623) – have been touched upon in this Introduction, and will inform our discussion of *Hamlet* and its characters at various points (most notably in Chapters 2 and 3). For detailed accounts of the textual history of *Hamlet*, and its significance for our understanding and appreciation of the play more generally, please consult the works cited in note 11 of this Introduction, and in the Further Reading and Bibliography.

CHAPTER 1

THE MAN IN BLACK: MEETING PRINCE HAMLET

This chapter considers how Shakespeare introduces us to Hamlet's character. What we learn of Hamlet at the beginning of the play – what might be termed our threshold experience of him in 1.2 – may well be crucial for how we read his character throughout the subsequent five acts. But it is also the aim of this chapter to address the complexities surrounding Hamlet's initial appearance. When do we first meet the Prince, for example? We see him for the first time in 1.2, but he is introduced, by name at least, at the end of 1.1, where Horatio and Marcellus agree to inform 'young Hamlet' about the Ghost they have seen, in the hope that 'This spirit dumb to us will speak to him' (1.1.170). Such a decision might seem innocuous enough. As 'old' Hamlet's son, whom the Ghost (we are told) resembles exactly, it is natural perhaps to tell 'young Hamlet' about it. But why not also inform old Hamlet's brother, the new king, of this supernatural occurrence, along with the dead king's former wife and queen, Gertrude? Hamlet's name, in other words, is conjured in 1.1 both in close conjunction with the Ghost's appearance (indeed, the identity of the former is inextricably bound-up with the existence of the latter from the very beginning) and in a context of some secrecy and uncertainty. 'Young Hamlet' is someone whom Marcellus and Horatio seem to trust: he is to be relied upon to provide a solution to the mystery of the Ghost (Palfrey, 284).

The Hamlet we meet in 1.2 appears, though, to be a very different character. By turns, he seems morose, taciturn, embittered, sarcastic, melancholy, sinister, even villainous. Hamlet's presence in 1.2 is distinctly shifty rather than trustworthy, signalling – like the Ghost of 1.1 – that all is not well in the world we have entered. Yet it is in just such movements of 'character', marked by contradiction and indirection as much as anything else, that we find our directions for reading Hamlet in 1.2. In this scene, it is as if we meet not just one but a series of Hamlets, who reveal different aspects of themselves as the action progresses, and which allows various dimensions of the Prince's character to unfold in surprising ways. Exactly when we can say we first meet the 'real' Hamlet becomes much trickier as a result.

THAT WITHIN

'Seems', madam – nay it is, I know not 'seems'.
'Tis not alone my inky cloak, cold mother,
Nor customary suits of solemn black,
Nor the windy suspiration of forced breath,
No, nor the fruitful river in the eye,
Nor the dejected haviour of the visage,
Together with all forms, moods, shapes of grief,
That can denote me truly. These indeed 'seem',
For they are actions that a man might play,
But I have that within which passes show,
These but the trappings and the suits of woe (1.2.76–86)

Is it with these words that we meet or see Hamlet's 'character' properly for the first time? We might be tempted to think so, as this is the first substantial speech Hamlet delivers in the play, and its importance as such has long been recognized. Here, we get our first taste of Hamlet's impressive rhetorical skills, beyond the cutting puns he has so far returned to the King and Queen in sharp, rapier-like hits. As his punningly 'inky cloak' might remind us, he is a figure whose natural element seems to be that of language. With great verbal virtuosity, his wordplay in 1.2 punctures courtly ceremony (refusing his uncle's claim on him as his 'son' by turning Claudius's sentiments into riddles); and yet he can discourse too with a graceful eloquence, all the while hiding himself squid-like behind a studied and 'inky' obscurity. 'Words, words, words' (2.2.189) will from the outset prove Hamlet's most secure means of defence and his sharpest weapons of choice.

The fact that the word 'seems' sparks Hamlet's first brief monologue in 1.2 invites us to read it as in some sense a statement about character: about seeming and being, appearance and perception, hypocrisy and authenticity. Hamlet's words align his character with an emotional core, 'that within', which goes beyond the mere outward 'show' of any 'trappings' and 'suits of woe', these being things that could never 'denote' him 'truly' in any case. Yet at the same time, this Hamlet also seems to be aware of the theatricality of selfhood and of the nature of identity as performative. The phrase 'actions that a man might play' introduces a defining trope in *Hamlet* to which Hamlet's theatrical mode of thinking will return again in the play (see Forker). In this speech, then, we see Hamlet declaring the existence of a private and secret self alongside an awareness of selfhood as something 'played'. It invites us to recognize Hamlet as possessing an inwardness or interiority – 'character' in that sense – which is simultaneously hidden from us and which remains too deep to fathom. We might see in these words a 'subjectivity' being spoken into existence (what Bloom refers to as the 'internalization of the self', a 'real interiority' (Bloom 1999, 409)), marking the very birth of modernity, of the psychological subject, as well as of post-modernity: of a decentred subject, shifty, unfixed, radical.

Before we get carried away by the revolutionary nature of Hamlet's 'that within', we should be wary of assuming that this speech bears any such coding of Hamlet's interiority. On one level, Hamlet's words suggest that he possesses something inward and hidden; but simultaneously they serve a much less romantic purpose: to turn our attention away from 'that within' him, and towards the public hypocrisy of others. This speech allows Hamlet to cast scorn on those whose signs of grief and mourning (dressing in 'customary' suits of grief, sighing in a 'forced' manner, with eyes teeming with conveniently 'fruitful' tears) are self-serving rather than sincere. Not only are these 'actions that a man' – or woman – 'might play', but by implication it is the newly crowned King and freshly remarried Queen who seem to have played them, in forgetting Hamlet's father so soon (as Hamlet's first soliloquy will make clear). Such a speech might reveal a Hamlet who is far from simply lost within himself, in a melancholy vein of introspection. This Hamlet is also a clever, bitter, satirical creature, intent upon poisoning the courtly scene at the centre of which he now stands. As yet, of course, we have no idea why he is behaving like this. But like the King, we may have our suspicions.

Our certainty that this speech tells us something important about Hamlet's 'true' inward character – 'that within' – starts to fall apart at the 'seems' when read as a subtle but pointed form of satirical attack by the Prince. But there are other reasons why there is more afoot than just a melancholy admission of that 'which passes show'. Could we view this speech as too controlled to be straightforwardly confessional, perhaps? Is it being delivered for courtly consumption, more than anything else? We might think so. Hamlet elaborates the implications of the word 'seems' very carefully, for example, as if it were a conceit or a curious term to be unpacked through witty disputation: it allows him to list the funereal 'actions that a man might play' with a display of rhetorical adeptness underscored by an accomplished use of anaphora (the cumulative repetition of 'Nor': 'Nor customary', 'Nor windy', 'nor the fruitful river', 'Nor the dejected haviour'). In an argument of demonstration and illustration that works steadily from the opening 'I know not "'seems'"' to the concluding 'These indeed "seem"' eight lines later, a rhyming couplet (pairing 'show' and 'woe') closes this metrically tight monologue with a polished and resolved finality. How certain can we be, then, that Hamlet is speaking from the heart: from 'that within'? It is as if Hamlet is bringing into being here a maimed sonnet on the subject of grief and 'seeming', as yet half-formed and unrhymed, but with its organizing idea and final couplet nevertheless already in place. As Edward Burns suggests, this 'very poised, public speech' indicates that Hamlet's 'interiority is in itself a series of rhetorical strategies' at this point (Burns, 141–2). For this reason, 'I know not seems' is markedly different (as we shall see) from the rougher, more unbalanced and more properly confessional outpourings of Hamlet's first soliloquy, given to us when he is at last left alone (1.2.129–59). Perhaps we do not meet the 'real' Hamlet, then, before we hear this first soliloquy, even when he appears to be declaring the existence of an authentic self: 'that within'.

LET THE DEVIL WEAR BLACK

The 'I know not seems' speech should not be read in isolation either: it marks the climax of a dramatic sequence through which the revelation of Hamlet's *persona* has been carefully staggered up to this point by Shakespeare. At the centre of his staged introduction is not the issue of 'that within', moreover, but of 'that without': how Hamlet is dressed. Whatever else we might speculate or infer, the one feature of Hamlet's character that cannot be denied or avoided is the blackness of his outfit: arguably, this is the single most important factor for us to consider when addressing how Shakespeare initially presents him. The dialogue that surrounds Hamlet in 1.2 reminds us of it strenuously. He is addressed first with a question about the 'clouds' that still 'hang' on him, and this opening series of exchanges leads into the 'I know not seems' speech as a means of reinforcing – even exaggerating – our awareness of Hamlet's 'inky cloak' and his 'suits of solemn black'. To have Hamlet dressed in anything other than this colour would be as absurd as the proverbial notion of performing *Hamlet* without the Prince. Hamlet's character is simply synonymous with what he is wearing: he is the definitive man in black – mysterious, intriguing, unknowable, sinister.

For a role famed for and defined by 'Words, words, words' (2.2.189), this emphasis on the visual composition of his character may seem ironic. It is, moreover, an aspect of Hamlet's characterization easy to overlook. On the page, Hamlet's outward appearance may register with much less impact than on stage or screen, and perhaps not at all. Literary criticism tends to take the written word as its starting point for interpretation, rather than engaging in the non-verbal business of costume and colour (Harris and Korda, 4–7; Bevington). As readers, we might gravitate towards Hamlet's words, and to that first major speech in particular, as a natural place to begin reading his character. But we do not meet Hamlet for the first time only when he speaks. He appears with the rest of the on-stage cast at the start of 1.2, but remains silent for around 64 lines, being offered no invitation to speak before then. The opening of 1.2 leaves Hamlet in a state of marginalized silence, and the audience in one of unsettling suspense. After all, what does the actor playing Hamlet do on stage during the first 60 or so lines? In performance, do we have Hamlet visibly present during this period of waiting, or hiding in shadows? If we knew nothing about this play at all, we might well be wondering: what is this man doing here? What's his problem?

What we cannot fail to notice about Hamlet in his silence, though, is what he is wearing: black. This feature is explicable partly in terms of dramatic impact, allowing Shakespeare to identify Hamlet as an outsider from the start, a figure isolated from the proceedings going on around him by his refusal to participate in the courtly world of Elsinore (Holmes, 83; Mercer, 141–2). His 'inky cloak', conspicuous in a scene often taken to be part of ongoing marriage celebrations and certainly as an occasion of state, identifies Hamlet as a figure of resentment and refusal. Although without yet knowing why, Hamlet's disapproval of Denmark's new regime and of his mother's remarriage is signalled by the shadows his 'clouds' cast over 1.2. By remaining in his mourning clothes, it is not just that Hamlet is refusing to come to terms with his father's death – the 'common' fact of life that his uncle and mother press him to accept – but the whole new set-up in his political and familial life. By wearing black, Hamlet becomes a visual and physical memento of his father's death, a living performance of remembrance, the spectacle of which throws a particularly effective spanner into the supposedly smooth-running machines of family and state. All of this before Hamlet even opens his mouth.

We can see instantly how Hamlet's costume intensifies our experience of first meeting *Hamlet*'s hero: he appears, before speaking, as a figure defined in the absence of words by a costume absent of colour. Yet it is what this blackness says about Hamlet's character – why he has chosen to remain in black even at his mother's wedding – that perhaps intrigues us most. It might indicate that Hamlet, a character whom we will see slipping between identities and roles with alarming ease and rapidity from 1.5 onwards, begins the play by attempting to *fix* his identity. In sticking to his 'suits of woe', it is as if the Hamlet we first meet in 1.2 is seeking a form of permanence, a means of 'identity maintenance' (Desmet 1992, 73), in the midst of the unsettling transitions with which the play begins. If Hamlet is now somehow his uncle's cousin *and* his son, not heir to his father's throne but Prince of Denmark still, then we are left to imagine a whole series of disturbing possibilities that crowd around Hamlet's initial identity. Could he have been Claudius's son all along, we might begin to wonder, as Harold Bloom suggests (Bloom 2003, 7–8)? How long have his mother and uncle been lovers? And would Hamlet still be heir apparent if his mother were to bear another child? In such a destabilizing psychological environment, how else can his identity be secured other than by fixing it as a self that vows never to cease mourning, never to forget, and never to change its appearance? As one commentator puts it, Hamlet's choice of clothing indicates how dress 'serves [. . .] to "stabilize identity"': 'Our outer dress does inner work for us, and if our clothes "mean", it is in the first place to ourselves', especially when it comes to resolving 'an uncertainty as to who or what we are.' In this sense, 'dressing involves people's fundamental sense of their selves': it is 'one way in which they construct their "subjectivities" '. In providing us with an identity, with a sense of self, clothes can 'save us from being lost' (Harvey, 14–18).

Yet, as much as we might see Hamlet 'conjuring a new persona' for himself in this way, his costume also works *against* fixing his identity, by inviting a plethora of other possible identifications associated with the colour of his clothes, all of which complicates how we decipher Hamlet's initial 'appearance messages' (Harvey, 13–14). As John Harvey notes, the colour black and the motives for wearing it can easily be misread, partly because its meanings are inherently 'multivalent' and accretive: they 'accrue, thickening over time by accretion of usage' (Harvey, 13). For example, black is the colour of grief in *Hamlet*, of remembering the dead; but it is also the colour of death itself, and of the bringer of death. Black is the colour of the night, in this respect, and so of the sinister, deadly, and demonic: it is the colour worn by villains and thieves, assassins and devils (as Hamlet reminds Ophelia when he proclaims, 'let the devil wear black, for I'll have a suit of sables' (3.2.122–3)). Yet it is also the colour of self-repression and ascetic renunciation: of Dominican friars, and of Puritan ministers alike. It is the colour of wealth and social respectability, that of fashionable Renaissance courtiers and of socially mobile merchants, as well as of the dissident or the rebel who seeks to resist the shallow changeability of fashions and to appear classless and outside any social and political order. As Harvey summarizes, black 'is a paradoxical colour, ostentatious through the show it makes of renouncing ostentation', and thereby allowing 'the man in black' to 'sidestep the social staircase because he seems to take his stand on a moral stair instead, and take the high ground through humility' (Harvey, 65).

We can see how Hamlet is exploiting black as 'a moral colour' in 1.2. Occupying the high ground seems to be the point of his first exchanges, and of his first major speech ('I know not seems'). But there is more to black as a 'paradox colour' than the way it frames the Prince either as a figure of moral conscience or as a sinister and 'honourably menacing' threat to the harmony of Elsinore (Harvey, 52). Perhaps more than anything else, black is the colour of self-effacement. Whether motivated by grief and mourning, by social dissidence or villainy, the purpose in dressing entirely in black is predominantly to negate one's 'self' (Harvey, 43). As Harvey notes, in European history black has always been 'the colour of loss, of negation, the colour with which one annuls one's self'. Dressing in black declares: 'Don't see me, and, See me' simultaneously. 'I show you here what is not to be seen', it says, and 'I am what is not. I am no self and sheer self'. Mediating 'between the conspicuous and that which is not to be seen', black 'is the very colour of "identity ambivalence" '. While 'the man in black, like the woman in white, is a whole family of personae', opening the wearer to a whole range of possible motives and inferences, it is also a means of fixing identity in paradox, because it is conspicuously the 'colour of invisibility', and most recognizably the 'colour of incognito'. It is the sign of 'denial and loss', but also of 'power over oneself': it is traditionally, then, 'the colour with which one buried one's self – the colour that having no colour, effaced and took away one's self', as well as the mark of 'impressive intense inwardness' (Harvey, 16, 52, 18, 93, 43, 46).

It is clear, in these terms, just how and why Hamlet will always 'remain current' as a role (Harvey, 101). His clothes identify him as the 1590s prince and the 1960s activist; as the avant-garde aristocrat, and the dissident university student; the adolescent 'Goth', and the grieving 30-something. The man in black, as we know from contemporary cinema, is permanently up-to-date: reliably dramatic, always relevant, always open to reinvention. But we can see too just how and why Shakespeare chooses to draw attention to Hamlet's 'inky cloak' and his 'suits of woe' so emphatically in 1.2. As a way of introducing Hamlet's character, nothing could communicate more effectively the idea of the Prince as a complex, ambiguous subject than the way he is dressed. What we learn in the process is that Shakespeare starts to generate the 'penumbra of inferences' about who and what Hamlet is – hero, or villain; puritan or devil – from 'without', and in a way continued throughout the play via the stage properties that orbit Hamlet's person, and which serve further to define and give life, depth, and complexity to his character. For if Hamlet's 'inky cloak' performs 'inner work', telling us something about who and what he might be, then so must his sword (which he seems to draw against his own friends in 1.4, and against Claudius in 3.3, and yet again in killing Polonius in 3.4); and the 'tables' in which he scribbles desperately after encountering the Ghost in 1.5; and the book he is reading when he enters in 2.2; and the dagger (the 'bare bodkin') that he perhaps contemplates as an instrument of suicide in the 'To be, or not to be' soliloquy; and – most famously of all – the skull he scrutinizes in the graveyard of 5.1. All of these silent objects speak powerfully of Hamlet's various roles and identities – scholar, soldier, courtier, as well as mourner, philosopher, murderer – constituting from without our varied sense of his character 'within' (see Charney 1965; Bevington, 35–66; Bruster 2002; Sofer 2003).

The gesture of holding Yorick's skull – the most famous theatrical prop of all time – has become visual shorthand for the whole of *Hamlet*, and understandably so. Where else do we learn more about Hamlet's identity (his age and when he was born, his childhood 'self', his suddenly recovered memories, as well as his destiny) than at this point? At what other moment do we approach Hamlet's character more intimately than when he gazes into this object of death and silence, as if it were a mirror reflecting not just his face but his fate? The mute skull offers an ominous visual pun on mutability, of course: it is Yorick's last joke, perhaps. But it also marks a climax in the play's unfolding of Hamlet's character through 'a silent language that speaks through properties' (Bruster 2002, 83–4), and which provides a visual *coda* for the play's recurring references to tongues and ears, and death and silence. The first articulation of this 'silent language' comes with Hamlet's blackness. It is Hamlet's clothing that first marks his 'dark ontology' (Harvey, 95), making his character from the outset a shadow's shadow, a darkness visible.

KIN, KIND, KING

Hamlet's decision to remain in black is 'at once perceived, both by the court and the audience, as dramatic and ominous, and involving more than grief' (Harvey, 92–3). Why, we are left to wonder with Claudius, is he still dressed like this? One inference to draw could be political: that Hamlet's blackness marks not just a continued mourning for his father (which we have no reason to doubt, on one level), but also a dissatisfaction with his own regal disappointment, or even dispossession. Young Hamlet's problem in 1.2, in other words, might simply be due to the fact that he is not wearing the crown, and that following the death of his father, he is still the prince, rather than the king of Denmark. There is much to suggest that Shakespeare has framed 1.2 to encourage such a reading. It would certainly explain something about Hamlet's initial display of alienation and resentment, both in appearance and in words, as well as why he is sidelined by Claudius from the outset, whose very first words seem either calculatedly or clumsily cruel in this respect. This scene's opening half-line – 'Though yet of Hamlet' (1.2.1) – clearly echoes Horatio's reference to 'young Hamlet' spoken just a few lines prior to this moment, at the end of 1.1, and it invokes the Prince's name and his destiny as the proper subject of the new king's first speech. Rather than explain or clarify Hamlet's position, though, Claudius raises courtly (and dramatic) interests and expectations only to disappoint them. It is of Hamlet 'our dear brother's death' that the King decides to address instead, while the living Hamlet, his 'cousin' and now also his 'son', must wait a further 63 lines to be considered. When Hamlet does first speak, moreover, it is with a line, half-proverb and half-riddle – he is, he says, 'A little more than kin, and less than kind' (1.2.65) – that both suggests and obscures his dissatisfactions. What on earth does he mean by this? Like his 'inky cloak', Hamlet's first words throw out some deeply unsettling ambiguities. Or do they? What if Hamlet's meaning is actually quite clear? As Simon Palfrey has suggested, perhaps this first line from Hamlet 'is a riddle with an answer'. More than 'kin', but less than 'kind': what else is Hamlet declaring himself to be here other than the rightful '*king*?' (Palfrey, 285–6)

The fact that we are also unsure about how or to whom an actor would deliver these words makes them even more ambiguous. In some editions of the play, Hamlet's first line is accompanied by a stage direction that turns it into an aside (making it private, sarcastic, comical even, rather than a defiant or openly challenging claim to the throne), a convention alien to the first printed versions of the play (the 1604/05 Second Quarto or the 1623 Folio texts), where no such 'aside' is indicated. Whether we have Hamlet speaking his opening riddle as a sly comment to the audience or to the other characters onstage, or delivering them straight to Claudius's face, these words serve to enact a deliberate breaking of decorum: Hamlet speaks them to interrupt the King and to puncture any pretence that all is well.

Hamlet's second line seems equally riddling, or at least just as punning, and is likewise open to personal, familial, and political interpretations. In stating 'I am too much in the "son"' (1.2.67), Hamlet sarcastically pushes back at Claudius his paternal attempt to address him as 'my son' just three lines earlier. But in doing so Hamlet draws attention both to the problem of his uncle's hasty marriage to his mother (Claudius's 'sometime sister' (1.2.8)), and to his own problematic identity not just as his uncle's cousin-and-son, but as a prince and heir who can lay claim, albeit ironically, to 'the sun' as a symbol of royalty and so of implied regal power – the very thing he is distinctly 'too much' without, perhaps. Crucially, this language of kin and kind, sons and suns may invite us to question not just the legitimacy of the marital union of Claudius and Gertrude, but also why, as the dead king's son, Hamlet has not inherited his father's title, which has evidently passed instead to old Hamlet's brother, Claudius. Our first question about 1.2 could thus be a straightforwardly pragmatic, political one: why *is not* young Hamlet – as son of old Hamlet – now king of Denmark?

This question certainly adds to what Harry Levin terms the dominant 'interrogative' mood and mode of *Hamlet*, a play which famously opens with a question – 'Who's there?' – and which proceeds to raise more and more questions as the drama progresses, without necessarily providing satisfactory answers (Levin, 17–43). What we are left with are possible alternatives, likely probabilities, and uncertain inferences. Why Hamlet has not inherited the throne upon his father's death according to the laws of inheritance that so firmly underscore, for instance, the politics of Shakespeare's earlier tragical history (or historical tragedy) *Richard II*, has been explained by scholars in a way both factually mundane and vitally important. The Denmark of *Hamlet* is an elective monarchy, it seems: while the ruler must have some claim to the throne – as both Claudius and Hamlet have, in their relations to the deceased king – nevertheless the king is elected to the throne only by decree of council (Honigmann 1963; de Grazia 2007, 81–107). The signs are all in place that this is so in *Hamlet*, for the King appears in 1.2 (according to the stage directions of the 1604/05 Second Quarto *Hamlet* at least) as if having come from a meeting of state council, before thanking all for their 'better wisdoms' (1.2.15) in approving his marriage to the former queen, an action that makes his position as ruler doubly secure: as 'imperial jointress' (1.2.9) it may be that Gertrude has some power to confer on Claudius this title (de Grazia 2007, 106–7; Jardine 1996, 35–47). Moreover, in the speech that follows, Claudius indicates that since his accession to the throne, young Fortinbras of Norway has been threatening war over 'those lands / Lost by his father [i.e. old Fortinbras] with all bands of law / To our most valiant brother [i.e. old Hamlet]' (1.2.16–25). What these lines make clear is that young Fortinbras is not king of Norway, despite his father, the previous king of Norway, having died (at the hands of Hamlet's father in combat, as we have by now been reminded twice, the first time by Horatio in 1.1.79–94). The king of Norway is identified by Claudius as the 'impotent and bedrid' uncle of Fortinbras, all of which suggests that the English political system of inheritance – from father to son – is not the norm in this part of the world, where uncles, whether in Norway or Denmark, have taken the throne instead.

But even with this notion of an elective monarchy in mind, the problem of Hamlet's dispossession – why he is not king – may not so easily be resolved for us. Whatever clues there are to indicate that Claudius has been elected as the rightful king in 1.2, the whole situation, as John Dover Wilson noted some time ago, might still strike any English audience – whether early modern or later – as politically rotten: 'There is something amiss here', he notes, as 'brothers do not succeed brothers, unless there is a failure in the direct line of succession' (31). The political drama of *Hamlet* is established (for Wilson, at least) as soon as Claudius appears in 1.2 wearing the crown: 'For if Shakespeare and his audience thought of the constitution of Denmark in English terms' (and he wonders why any audience would imagine 'a different constitution from themselves'), then the situation becomes obvious: '*Hamlet was the rightful heir to the throne and Claudius a usurper*' (Wilson, 30, 36). The dramatic impact of 1.2, in other words, rests in part upon our awareness of Hamlet as a disinherited son and prince, so that Hamlet's initial quibbling and riddling signal 'disappointed hopes of succession': 'Hamlet's bitterness' in 1.2 thus points directly to 'his exclusion from the throne' (Wilson, 30–8).

Margreta de Grazia has recently revived such a reading, arguing that we are bound to be misled in our understanding both of the play and the character of Hamlet if we fail to recognize him as 'dispossessed' or as part of the 'patronymic' sequence of the play as a whole. For de Grazia, 'Hamlet had every reason to expect to succeed his father' and 'to grieve inordinately' given that when we meet him in 1.2 'he has lost more than a father', having inherited 'nothing of his father's estate' (de Grazia 2007, 86–7). But de Grazia does not dismiss the relevance of the Danish constitution as an elective monarchy in *Hamlet*, unlike Wilson, who sees it as nothing more than a 'mirage' (Wilson, 38). De Grazia notes that, on the one hand, 'Even in an elective monarchy, like that of Denmark up until 1660–1, succession tended to pass from father to son', while on the other,

'Denmark's electoral constitution is crucial to the play's dramatic set-up' in any case, as it 'allows for a situation impossible in a primogenitary monarchy', or in any of Shakespeare's English chronicle plays, for that matter: one in which 'the Prince remains at court in company of the King who was preferred over him' (de Grazia 2007, 83, 88–9).

We can see just how and why Shakespeare would have seized the dramatic potential of such a tense political environment, and of the conflicts – political, psychological, familial – that could arise from a stage occupied simultaneously by rightful king and dispossessed heir (with all of this being complicated further by Hamlet's mother's rapid remarriage). Yet, for our purposes, the most far-reaching implications of this situation concern character, as a curious doubling effect is produced by the way the court scene of 1.2 is dominated by the rival royal figures of the loquacious Claudius and the silent, then riddling, Hamlet. We might instinctively assume, with John Dover Wilson, and with a whole tradition of readers and critics stretching back to Samuel Johnson, that Claudius is a usurper (and therefore tyrant and despot), and that Hamlet is the just and rightfully indignant dispossessed heir. From this perspective, Hamlet's indecorous opening quips and quiddities, along with his conspicuously inappropriate black garb, might be viewed as signs of a righteous dissidence, and a witty but soulful resistance of wrongful rule and imposed tyranny. Yet, when viewed from the perspective of a Danish elective constitution, Hamlet's opening words might suggest something quite different, and much more obscure morally. As a rightful heir deprived of the throne by a process duly legal and constitutional, making Claudius king by an election bolstered by his marriage to the former king's wife, how else might Hamlet's demeanour, verbally and visually, be understood other than as insolent, threatening, sinister and even treasonous? How else might Hamlet first appear in 1.2 other than as a malcontent prince, whose eye is set upon the crown, and whose heart, even when proclaimed by Claudius as 'most immediate to our throne' still, might be given over to much darker aspirations and ambitions? By this point in *Hamlet*, we have no idea yet that Claudius has obtained the crown by foul deeds and horrible murder: he may seem, for all intents and purposes, the constitutionally correct king. If we have neither read *Hamlet* nor seen it performed before, could this prince be a black-hearted villain, we might wonder: a character who openly confesses to being 'less than kind'? What else might the 'nighted colour' of his clothes imply? What if 'that within which passes show' were really a political, even murderous desire to seize the crown for himself?

HAMLET'S FIRST SOLILOQUY

Although Hamlet's political ambitions and disaffections resurface periodically in hints and revelations throughout *Hamlet* (most notably, for example, in 5.2.63–4), we could still read the Prince of 1.2 as something other than a potential villain: as the 'Good Hamlet' (1.2.68) that his mother and his uncle-stepfather-king describe him as. This is a man who has taken his father's death too much 'to heart', as Claudius puts it, and who is being mistakenly 'obstinate', 'unmanly', and 'peevish' in his display of grief (as Claudius's speech at 1.2.87–117 suggests). This is certainly more like the Hamlet whom we first meet in Laurence Olivier's 1948 film, though it is worth noting how much work Olivier (as the film's director) has to do to make Hamlet fit this threshold image of him as the 'man who could not make up his mind'. Not only must Olivier frame Hamlet as such from the outset, introducing him through this famous description in voice-over at the very beginning of the film, but 1.2 is both cut and shot by Olivier in such a way as to remove any politically threatening features from Hamlet's first appearance. Olivier's cinematic Hamlet sidesteps his first two sarcastic, politically loaded lines by omitting them completely, and we see him for the first time only when the camera reveals him sat in a suitably melancholy pose, uttering his first words (which in this adaptation are now, 'Ay, madam, it is common'). A strenuous effort has been made, in other words, to make Olivier's Hamlet politically disinterested rather than dangerously disaffected in 1.2, a move reinforced by the decision to cut the roles of Rosencrantz and Guildenstern as well as of young Fortinbras from the film, thus removing some of the most important vehicles through which Shakespeare articulates, or at least suggests, Hamlet's political identity, and his place within a world of courtly intrigue and international diplomacy.

As we have seen, the Hamlet of 1.2 could be much more complex and potentially dangerous than this. Up to Hamlet's first soliloquy, we may well be convinced that Hamlet's role is stereotypically fixed, as the black-habited, politically ambitious young malcontent: a villain not so dissimilar at heart, perhaps, from the misanthropic mischief-maker of *Much Ado About Nothing*, Don John. If we knew nothing at all about either Hamlet or *Hamlet*, either in terms of its plot or its sources, this is certainly the impression we might have of his 'character' at this point. It is for this reason that Hamlet's first soliloquy subsequently strikes us as so astonishing. By rights, what we should expect from our first time alone with Hamlet, certainly based on the way that Shakespeare has framed him so far, is a speech either of villainous frustration or of righteous indignation over being dispossessed of crown and kingdom: something treasonous and murderous, perhaps, but voicing something surely of his political loss. Yet we get nothing of the sort. Hamlet's first soliloquy opens not with any talk of plotting against Claudius, nor even with any complaint about his new position as 'chiefest courtier', but – stunningly – with desperate talk of 'self-slaughter' (1.2.132), in lines that constitute the dark prayer of a man consumed by despair: 'O God, God, / How weary, stale, flat and unprofitable / Seem to me all the uses of this world!' (1.2.132–4). Just as surprisingly, it is his mother who becomes the focus of this speech, rather than his uncle, with Hamlet's moral disgust being pointed away from his own political disappointment, and instead at his mother's hasty remarriage ('yet within a month', he reminds us three times) and its 'incestuous' implications (ll. 145, 147, 153, 157). Hamlet's first soliloquy, in other words, marks a genius move by Shakespeare in the characterization of his hero. Having prepared his audience for the plotting of a politically dispossessed young prince, Shakespeare gives us instead the soliloquy of a different character almost entirely – not coolly political, logical, and ruthless (as his opening exchanges in 1.2 might otherwise suggest), but intensely desperate and emotional, almost to the point of incoherence. Shakespeare plays a brilliant trick on us here when it comes to Hamlet's character: he trips us up; he wrong-foots us.

Such misdirection has not gone unnoticed. John Dover Wilson spotted that 'Hamlet makes no reference to the succession in the first soliloquy', having 'suffered' it seems 'a more overwhelming wrong in the degrading incestuous marriage of his mother'. This 'unexpected revelation' must hit spectators hard because it comes 'just when they were looking for something else', and so marks 'a master stroke, the first of many' in a play 'noteworthy' for its 'quality of surprise' (Wilson, 33–4). But the soliloquy may not be entirely devoid of political content. Margreta de Grazia has argued that Hamlet's dismay at his mother's speedy remarriage – the subject that comes to dominate this soliloquy – is in itself politically rather than psychologically determined. For it is the Queen's special status as 'imperial jointress' (1.2.9) to the realm, as Claudius first describes her at the beginning of 1.2, that signals Gertrude's power to 'settle the realm on her husband' following her first husband's death (de Grazia 2007, 105). If this were the case, then it might explain why Hamlet is so upset at her hasty second wedding. In marrying again as 'jointress', she guarantees that the crown will pass to Claudius, and thereby 'has alienated her son from what even in an elective monarchy would have been considered his birthright' (de Grazia 2007, 106, and see also Jardine 1983, 92–3).

The political Hamlet seems to be back in the running, then. Yet whatever the implications of Gertrude's hasty remarriage might be, frustration over non-succession still does not seem to be at the heart of Hamlet's first soliloquy. As such, de Grazia's brilliant argument does not really explain anything about why this speech has such immediate, dramatic impact. But perhaps nothing can prepare us for the first soliloquy. There is so much to surprise us in it, to seize our ears, that anything political must temporarily be put to one side as we deal with its emotional shifts and turns. The soliloquy's initial revelation of Hamlet's despair, for instance, makes the opening lines become a black orison of hopelessness as Hamlet cries 'O God, God' for his 'sallied' (or is it 'solid', or even 'sullied'?) 'flesh' to melt into a final nothingness: into an everlasting 'adieu' as much as 'a dew' (1.2.129–32).[1] Such desperate words align Hamlet's first soliloquy ominously with the final outcries (also in soliloquy, also in despair) of that other great Renaissance stage villain-hero: Christopher Marlowe's Dr Faustus (like Hamlet, a scholar of Wittenberg).[2]

But it is how the soliloquy turns suddenly upon the thought 'That it should come thus' (l. 137) that startles us most, partly because what Hamlet reveals next is the intensity of his disgust at his mother's marriage to his uncle, and partly because that disgust in itself is enacted through the shaping of the verse. Hamlet's lines become markedly broken and unhinged at this point, both grammatically (he seems no longer able to articulate his thoughts in complete sentences) and metrically (as he seems incapable of speaking in a consistently measured iambic pentameter). Instead, this soliloquy becomes schizometric, with the lines stretching anywhere between eight syllables (l. 149) and 15 syllables (l. 140), making it seem something like a hybrid: neither prose nor verse, but something unsteadily between. We might see another wry connection to the parody of

Hamlet as the footman in *Eastward Ho* here. When left alone to speak in soliloquy (and in marked difference to the measured, rhetorical slickness of his public 'I know not seems' speech), Hamlet cannot keep his poetic feet together: he is distinctly unsteady when it comes to sticking to the iambic pentameter of his dramatic blank verse. But the effect of all this is powerful, instant, seemingly spontaneous. It communicates, with astonishing immediacy, the twists and turns of Hamlet's tortured thinking: bitter, unstable, almost unspeakable. The first soliloquy surprises us not just because it articulates the words of a man who must 'hold his tongue', and whose 'heart' will 'break' (1.2.159), but because it offers such a striking imitation of humanity from start to finish: it is unpredictable, unfinished, fragmented, and so nothing like the 'character' we may have expected Hamlet to be up to this point.

ON THE RUN AGAIN

To return to our initial question: is it in his first soliloquy that we properly meet the 'real' Prince Hamlet? One might, with more confidence perhaps, think so. Although the rest of the play teaches us to distrust the soliloquy as a device that guarantees unobstructed access to 'that within' Hamlet (as we shall see in the following chapter), nevertheless his first soliloquy establishes a series of issues and rhetorical motifs that will resurface throughout the play, underscoring the Prince's dramatic relationship to those around him, and in particular to the Ghost, Claudius and Gertrude. Perhaps the problem that this first soliloquy leaves us with, however, is that it also unveils a Hamlet with whom we might find it difficult to identify or fully sympathize. While Shakespeare has composed this speech in order for it to have as much of a direct and directly emotive impact as possible, nevertheless the focus of Hamlet's intensity here can be hard to accommodate. As T.S. Eliot famously put it: 'Hamlet is up against the difficulty that his disgust is occasioned by his mother, but that his mother is not an adequate equivalent for it', and so 'Hamlet (the man) is dominated by an emotion which is inexpressible, because it is in excess of the facts as they appear' (Eliot, 101). We may be baffled, then, by the sheer force of Hamlet's response to his mother's hasty remarriage. It may seem 'unmanly' in the sense that it marks something adolescent in Hamlet: appropriate more to a teenager than a prince. But we are also confronted by what appears to be Hamlet's misogyny, particularly in the famous phrase, 'Frailty, thy name is Woman' (1.2.146), and by the way he aligns his revulsion with his mother's sexual voracity: her 'appetite' is to blame (1.2.144).

As we know from Hamlet's subsequent interactions with both Gertrude and Ophelia, this 'distaste for sexuality' (and female sexuality in particular, one might think) will recur in various displays throughout the play, in such a way as to make Sigmund Freud pay attention to it as a significant aspect of his character (Freud, 368). Similarly, it is Hamlet's categorization of his mother's marriage to his uncle as 'incestuous' (1.2.157) that might, to our modern ears, strike an uncomfortably discordant note. Much has been written on the status of the marriage in *Hamlet* as 'incestuous', making it one of the key questions the play forces us to consider: and it certainly casts light on Hamlet's initial sarcasm with Claudius in declaring himself, 'more than kin, and less than kind'. Various scholars have explained that marrying one's brother's widow was outlawed in early modern England (it was illegal – or at least not considered valid – until 1921, in fact), on the basis of 'affinity' rather than 'consanguinity' (being members of the same family through marriage, that is, rather than being related by blood). This in itself helps perhaps to put into perspective Hamlet's outrage, indignation, and moral abhorrence.[3] Yet Hamlet's objection to the marriage on what may seem to be a primarily religious basis (the Scriptural verses forbidding a man to marry his wife's brother being Leviticus 18.16 and 20.21, cited in *Hamlet* 2006a, 179, n.157) may also seem to us quite puritanical. As such, what might strike us most uncomfortably about the tone of Hamlet's first soliloquy, revealing a Hamlet we may well prefer not to see, is its moral puritanism. This is a Hamlet who is, after all, reviled by sexuality and who sees the world as 'an unweeded garden', who prays to 'God, God' in his despair, and who condemns self-righteously his mother's 'unrighteous tears' and her 'incestuous sheets' (1.2.154, 157). Is Hamlet's first soliloquy the outpouring of grief from a man evidently suffering from melancholy, or the expression of an Oedipus complex? Or are these the words of a strictly religious man, a Protestant who studies at the University of Wittenberg (the home not just of Faustus, of course, but of Luther, the father of the Reformation)?[4]

Is Hamlet's 'inky cloak' one of devilish villainy and political ambition, then, or the costume of the Protestant pulpit? Could it be the mark of a distinctly Puritan 'cast of spirituality', signalled by the 'sartorial authoritarianism' of its black-garbed ministers and preachers (Harvey, 87–8)? Again, one might be tempted to think so. Given the way that Hamlet both warms to the Ghost's similarly condemnatory language in 1.5, and then harries his mother's soul so fiercely in 3.4 in the very terms given to us in the soliloquy of 1.2, it certainly looks as though Hamlet considers himself authorized to harass those around him like 'a righteous black-clad priest' (Harvey, 93). The problem as ever, though, is that Hamlet overturns such easy (or perhaps uneasy) categorizations and identifications almost as quickly as we are tempted to conclude upon them. In 1.2, what may be viewed as Hamlet's puritanism is countered instantly by the introduction of yet another 'Hamlet', the friendly fellow who emerges from beneath his cloak of sorrows when greeted by Horatio and Marcellus as his first soliloquy finishes, and who becomes himself (his true self, even?) yet again, we might think. Witty, urbane, comical even, yet honest and trustworthy, here is the friend and scholar whom we have been waiting to meet since this pair mentioned him at the end of 1.1. Is this, then, the 'real' Hamlet?

If so, then what about the Hamlet whose life and mind are irrevocably changed by the terrible duty placed upon him by the Ghost in 1.5? Hamlet enters the second act of the play having sworn himself into an 'antic disposition' (1.5.170), which will make it practically impossible to know whether we are seeing the 'real' Hamlet or not. But we can hardly be surprised by this idea, for our dramatic experience of his 'character' throughout the first act, and especially in 1.2, is one of misdirection and adjustment, as Hamlet reveals himself differently according to whom he is talking, where he is, whether he is alone, or whether others assume that he thinks he is alone. 1.2 establishes the pattern, then, for the unfolding of Hamlet's character throughout the play, and especially in the dramatic carousel of a scene such as 2.2, in which any actor playing Hamlet is tested to the full, as he switches his roles to suit the parade of characters that passes before him across the stage (Polonius, Rosencrantz and Guildenstern, the troupe of players, and Polonius again), and all before he speaks another long soliloquy, beginning suitably (and ironically) with 'Now I am alone' (2.2.484). If Hamlet were not to unfold in such a way, though, how else could we explain why it is as if we meet him for the first time yet again in 5.1, when he communes with Yorick's skull, or again in 5.2, when he tells Horatio how he sent Rosencrantz and Guildenstern ingeniously to their deaths? Is this murderous Hamlet really the 'sweet Prince' of Horatio's elegiac 'Goodnight' at the end of *Hamlet* (5.2.343)? When do we meet this 'sweet Prince'? Do we ever get to meet him? Even at the very end of the play, Hamlet's 'character' – this 'sweet Prince', this stranger – retains its remarkable momentum: it has a capacity to outrun us, even in death.

CHAPTER 2

HERO, VILLAIN, FOOL: THE CHARACTER OF HAMLET'S REVENGE

Hamlet remains throughout *Hamlet* as he first appears in 1.2: an *omnigatherum,* collecting in his person something of everything, and playing his numerous roles against one another in brilliant succession. He is the sophisticated thinker and the powerless politician; the resentful child and the sober student; the moral Puritan and the deranged Prince; the witty murderer and the cold-blooded jester. To this degree, Hamlet appears to be an archetypal Renaissance figure. Like the English courtier-soldier-poet Sir Philip Sidney or the Italian artist-technologist-anatomist Leonardo da Vinci, Shakespeare's Hamlet is a multi-talented creature: an educated prince-philosopher, a cultured courtier-player, a ferocious fighter-rhetorician. But he is also a Renaissance man in the way exemplified rather less reputably by the notorious Elizabethan writer and dramatist Robert Greene, described by his contemporary, Gabriel Harvey, as 'a wilde head, ful of mad braine', 'A scholler, a Discourser, a Courtier, a ruffian, a Gamester, a Louer, a Souldier [. . .] a Player, a Coosener, a Rayler [. . .] a Gay nothing [. . .] an Epitome of fantasticalitie'. This dizzying description of Greene, 'a Maister of Arte with ruffianly hair', provides an equally telling analogy for Hamlet's variety as a compendium of selves: an early modern man of no fixed identity.[1]

By the close of *Hamlet's* first Act, though, another crucial title has been added to his list of parts: that of avenger, or revenge hero, this being the role bequeathed to the Prince by the Ghost in commanding him to 'Revenge his [father's] foul and most unnatural murder' (1.5.25). The purpose of this chapter is to consider the effect this duty of revenge has upon Hamlet's character. Although revenge gives Hamlet a clear role (that of avenging son) as well as a direct course of action (he knows he must now 'set [. . .] right' these 'out

50

of joint' times (1.5.186–7) and avenge the 'foul deeds' over which he voices suspicions at the close of 1.2), nevertheless it complicates rather than clarifies our sense of his 'character'. Any initial uncertainty we might have about Hamlet's ethical identity in 1.2, for instance, is intensified by 'revenge' as a course of action that simultaneously draws us to and alienates us from him: as a 'revenger', Hamlet is transformed instantly into both hero and villain. Can a revenge hero become anything other than a murderer? In which case, how can he be any better than his enemies? Equally, revenge gives Hamlet leave temporarily to obliterate his sense of self at the end of Act 1 by allowing him to adopt an 'antic disposition': a mask of madness and tomfoolery that exaggerates and accelerates changes in his identity throughout the rest of the play. In the process, we often lose sight of Hamlet's 'character' amid his 'antic' performance. When, we might wonder, is Hamlet feigning madness, and when has he slipped into something beyond pretence? When does he speak as 'himself' after 1.5? And are his antics part of a strategy for taking revenge, or a means of postponing it?

If we were expecting revenge to fix the ambiguous Hamlet of 1.2 into a more secure and certain subject position, then we are proved mistaken. Revenge does not unify Hamlet's 'character': it fragments it even further. It makes him a hero with a task to perform, but in the process it turns him into a plotting villain and an unlicensed fool. While this kind of fragmentation follows a generic precedent set by a revenge drama such as Thomas Kyd's *The Spanish Tragedy* (possibly written during the late 1580s) – the sympathetic protagonist of which, Hieronimo, goes mad in avenging the murder of his son, Horatio – nevertheless our responses to Hamlet from this point onwards are defined by the duty he is now required to perform, as well as by the other ghost that has traditionally haunted him: the spectre of his 'delay'. *Hamlet* subsequently invites us to consider the term 'hero' as another complex form of dramatic identity that sits uneasily upon Hamlet's shoulders, as a hero allegedly incapable of heroic action.

While the focus here will be upon the character of Hamlet's revenge – that is, its particular quality and mode – nevertheless it is not Hamlet's 'character' alone that is under scrutiny in this chapter, but the broader machinery of *Hamlet*, in terms of the play's use of soliloquy and how it contributes to our sense of Hamlet's character and the action (as well as the inaction) of his revenge, and in relation also to the play's likely sources (and of *Hamlet*'s deviations from them), as well as the textual alternatives *Hamlet* offers (in the Second Quarto and Folio versions). There is much more to the character of Hamlet's revenge, and to Hamlet as a character of revenge, than just the mystery of 'that within', particularly when it comes to thinking about his infamous 'delay'.

I TO HERCULES

In the first soliloquy of 1.2 we are given what might seem an important clue about Hamlet's unsuitability for the task that the Ghost will set him just a few scenes later. In voicing despair over his mother's 'incestuous' marriage 'with my uncle', Hamlet compares his father to Claudius as being no more alike than 'Hyperion to a satyr' (1.2.140), and then states again, more crucially, that his 'father's brother' is 'no more like my father / Than I to Hercules' (1.2.152–3). This reference is important: it invites us to see Hamlet from the start as a hero who seems fully conscious of himself as relatively unheroic, perhaps even unmasculine. The allusion to Hercules has been carefully positioned by Shakespeare to conjure a conventional notion of 'a brave & masculine virtue' (as Ben Jonson summarizes Hercules's heroic qualities (Wells 2000, 26)), in the absence of which Hamlet conveys his own measure of himself as a man. A hero of 'inordinate passions and exceptional physical prowess', and held in high esteem in Renaissance art and thought, Hercules could be considered the archetypal man of action, 'associated above all with success in battle' and with establishing 'order' through 'physical conquest' (Wells 2000, 25–7). Symbolized by his weapon, a massive club, often depicted with the skin of the Nemean lion draped loosely over a muscle-rippling physique, and famed for his legendary completion of numerous impossible labours, the name of Hercules establishes an early and sharply ironic point of contrast when reading Hamlet's *persona*, and an important basis from which to see how Hamlet fares in his own Herculean labour: that of avenging his father's murder.

As a self-consciously un-Herculean hero, this allusion alone might explain a great deal about Hamlet's subsequent actions, as well as what might be perceived as inaction. Should we see Hamlet, for instance, as physically weak? Is he the 'unmanly' and 'peevish' figure Claudius hints at, after all? Is he just melancholy, or cowardly? Should we see Hamlet, in other words, as an anti-heroic figure from the start, who privileges the workings of the mind (and of the tongue) over the actions of the body, as we might well expect of our sensitive student of Wittenberg: a master of the liberal rather than the martial arts? Hamlet is different not just from Hercules in this respect, but also from his own father, the old Hamlet who defeated the king of Norway in single combat, and whose Ghost appears in full battledress in 1.2 and 1.4–1.5, as if to remind us of this feat (see Foakes 2005). This notion of an un-Herculean Hamlet can be misleading, though, as Hamlet's deflating, matter-of-fact description also seems ironic. It is hard to reconcile any self-confessed effeminacy or heroic inadequacy with the character who proves throughout the play to be as adept physically as he is verbally, who threatens to kill his companions in 1.4 should they stand in his way (becoming 'As hardy as the Nemean lion's nerve' at this point, no less (1.4.83)), and who wrestles with Laertes in the graveyard of 5.1 and then matches him at swordplay in 5.2, managing to kill Claudius before dying himself (having escaped death prior to his return in Act 5, we should not forget, by jumping aboard a pirate ship amid a fierce sea-skirmish). Such are not the actions of a sensitive flower.

But as physical and as aggressive as Hamlet can actually appear, his negative assessment of himself as whatever Hercules is not has remained, for centuries, one of the dominant ways of regarding Hamlet as a 'hero'. As we explored in the Introduction, Romantic commentators in particular preferred to frame Hamlet as a figure of cerebral rather than physical prowess: a man who thinks rather than acts, and whose chief characteristic trait – his thoughtfulness, his propensity to philosophize himself out of action and into procrastination and delay – marks him as a being far superior in sensibility to any run-of-the-mill stage-revenger. Such views can be difficult to counter, moreover, given that the play itself seems to invite such a reading at times. The way that Hamlet first responds to the Ghost's call for revenge, for example, is notably ambivalent. The Prince does not delay in accepting his task, desiring to know with 'Haste' the details of his father's 'Murder', so that 'I with wings as swift / As meditation or the thoughts of love / May sweep to my revenge', he states (1.5. 29–31). Yet the very language he uses in articulating this will-to-revenge (those 'wings [. . .] of meditation' and 'thoughts of love') marks Hamlet as less 'apt' (1.5.31) for the job than either we or the Ghost might at first expect. As Peter Mercer puts it: 'Hamlet may mean to speak of fearful intention and of ruthless speed' when he pronounces these lines, 'but what his language does is promptly undermine both.' Missing from Hamlet's response is 'the strenuous rhetoric of blood that is actually required for the acting of revenge' (Mercer, 166). What we get instead is a complex grouping of terms that might exemplify the un-Herculean nature of Hamlet's character more than anything else: his 'Haste me to know't' and his desire to 'sweep to my revenge' are offset and upset by what might seem an underlying characteristic preference for 'meditation'.

A similar effect is perceptible in Hamlet's behaviour as soon as the Ghost leaves the stage in 1.5. In the soliloquy that follows, Hamlet's language is shaped neither by the stage-assassin's ruthlessness, nor by rhetorical efficiency and cold logic, nor by the fire of injustice and outrage, but instead by a more profound and personal sense of horror, marked by his staggered meditation upon the Ghost's last words: 'remember me'. Hamlet's second soliloquy might seem even more fragmented and spontaneous than that of 1.2, for this reason: it breaks into articulation uneasily, erupting phrase by phrase and line by line as if from the mind of someone who has not only seen a ghost, but whose deepest fears and suspicions (of the 'foul play' and 'foul deeds' of which he speaks at the close of 1.2) have been realized, and whose once secure view of the world is now imploding. This is a speech full of outbursts and questions, then, from 'O earth' and 'O fie!' (1.5.92–93) to 'My tables!' (l. 107), and from 'what else?' (l. 92) to 'Remember thee? [. . .] Remember thee?' (ll. 95, 97). But the references to 'memory' and to 'remembering' also indicate that revenge is pushing Hamlet not outwards or forwards into action here, but backwards and inwards: into the realm of 'memory' and into the 'distracted globe' of his own head, 'the book and volume' of his 'brain' (ll. 97, 103). Hamlet's first act as revenger seems telling in this respect. The first thing Hamlet does is write a memo to himself, not just in 'the table of my memory' (l. 98) but in his actual 'tables' (usually thought to be a notebook or diary of some sort). This is an action that might signal a concern not with revenge but over 'that within', with memory and remembrance, and with a sudden urge to record his discovery 'That one may smile and smile and be a villain' (l. 108). As such, Hamlet's agitated note-making in 1.5 could be construed as a sign of 'radical reflexivity' rather than any capacity to revenge: it seems to be the action of a diarist or a journal-keeper, of an introspective self rather than of a cunning revenger (Lee, 199–200).

What is most startling about the small but significant action of Hamlet writing in his tables, though, is just how naturalistic it seems: it is just the kind of thing a human being would do in a state of shock. Hamlet, the scholar of Wittenberg, when confronted by a Ghost that tells him of his father's murder and that commands him both to 'Revenge' and to 'remember me' (and, impossibly, not to 'taint' his 'mind' while so doing (1.5.85)), does first what he knows how to do best, we might think. He makes a note of something, he writes something down, thereby turning the Ghost's instructions – and his own experience – bookishly into something more familiar: a text to be studied and learned. Thoughts of tombs turn quickly into tomes, and those of villains into volumes. Such automatic behaviour may seem neither logical nor useful nor appropriate from a revenge hero, but it is strangely realistic as an imitation of humanity. It is an unthinking response: an immediate act of 'identity maintenance' from someone whose Herculean job it now is to bear the burdens of a world that seems suddenly to have become radically deranged, and to set it all 'right' again.

Freud might have seen the business with Hamlet's tables as a classic display of 'perseveration', whereby deep feelings of trauma or crisis are directed into inconsequential, seemingly meaningless and repetitive or distracted actions, yet which remain significant by permitting 'impulses that are otherwise hidden to be revealed'.[2] We could imagine that Hamlet's writing in his tables marks the keynote in a drama characterized by 'perseveration': by repetition, inconsequential action, and meaningless fuss. But at the same time, the breakdown of Hamlet's identity that we witness following the soliloquy of 1.5 – as Hamlet falls into 'wild and whirling words' (1.5.132) with Horatio and Marcellus, swearing them to silence while dancing them around the stage to the tune of the Ghost's ghastly voice – might also be expected of the stage-revenger whose destiny is to become, as Mercer puts it, 'a spectacle of loss', and whom the action of revenge decomposes in tragic ways. If revenge metamorphoses 'the good man' into the 'pitiless revenger' and madman, then we can see this process beginning at the close of 1.5, both before and during Hamlet's decision to 'put on' a self-erasing 'antic disposition' (Mercer, 5–6, 21, 35).

In these terms, the initial act of hesitation or 'delay' that we might wish to read into Hamlet's second soliloquy might say less about his 'character' or 'that within' than it does about his dramatic function as a revenge hero, whose line of action is defined from the start (as we explored in the Introduction's discussion of 3.3) by 'delay'. Because stage-revenge must always involve the working out of 'cunning plots and secret devices of death', operating largely by indirection rather than through direct 'heroic' action, then 'the delay virtually *is* the action' in revenge tragedy: the question of revenge tragedy is never whether 'to revenge or not to revenge', but rather when to revenge, and how. Hamlet's hesitations and perseverations are not a problem for the enactment of revenge in *Hamlet*: they remain, rather, an essential part of it, becoming 'crucial to its structure of meaning' (Mercer, 2–4).

NOW I AM ALONE

We can now start to re-think the purpose and significance of the most prominent feature of *Hamlet*, and the aspect of the play's design which, perhaps more than anything else, might encourage us to view Hamlet as an inadequate hero, a reluctant revenger, and a hopeless procrastinator: his soliloquies. It is easy to see how and why Hamlet's capacity to soliloquize – to speak, that is, either to himself (as if thinking out loud) or directly to the audience (confiding in it alone his plans and fears), or perhaps combining something of the two – has particular and sometimes curious effects on our perception of his 'character'. The fact that Hamlet so often speaks in soliloquy (at least six or seven times before the close of Act 4), and usually at considerable length (anywhere between 12 and 56 lines), may give the distinct impression that he is indeed someone who prefers to talk and to think rather than to get on with revenge, and who substitutes words and thoughts for actions whenever he can. It would be to Hamlet's soliloquies that we might turn first and foremost, presumably, when characterizing him as a man who suffers from the habit of thinking too much, or from not being able to make up his mind.

Hamlet's own statements would seem to support such a view. The soliloquies of 2.2 and 4.4, for example, offer classic instances of Hamlet berating himself as a 'rogue and peasant slave' (2.2.485), a 'rascal' and a 'coward' (ll. 502, 506) for not having yet 'fatted all the region kites' with Claudius's 'offal' (ll. 514–15), and (much later again) for still not knowing why his 'revenge' has become so 'dull', other than through 'Bestial oblivion', perhaps, or from 'thinking too precisely on th'event' (4.4.31–45). The most famous soliloquy of all – 'To be, or not to be' of 3.1 – seems to suggest the same line of thinking. As a meditation on death and that fearful 'undiscovered country' (3.1.78) beyond, the central notion that 'conscience does make cowards' and that 'the native hue of resolution' is all too often 'sicklied o'er with the pale cast of thought', leaving 'enterprises of great pitch and moment' to 'lose the name of action' (ll. 82–7), may appear to address Hamlet's situation directly, as an avenger who does seem unable to take his revenge because he simply thinks too much about it, having 'quartered' every 'thought' along the way (4.4.41). At such moments he appears to be confessing, we might think, his characteristic weakness: he can think and talk but he cannot act, though neither he nor we seem entirely sure why.

By pausing the action so regularly, and by invoking a language mindful of delay, the soliloquies may appear to slow the momentum of the play considerably, stopping the plot in order to make way for a different kind of drama altogether: one of thought and conscience, of hesitation and procrastination, rather than one performed in 'the name of action' (3.1.87). In this sense, we can see just how crucial the soliloquies have been in the development of theories about Hamlet's character that seek to explain his 'delay' as a mark either of his delicate sensibility as a thinker and a philosopher, or as a sign of a psychological flaw of some kind. After all, Hamlet does not hesitate through any concern over the moral or ethical problems of revenge. His dilemma is not one of 'conscience' in that sense. He never worries that revenge may not be the right path to take, but accepts his task from the Ghost unquestioningly in 1.5, and never regrets having done so. Far from appearing squeamish or uncertain about such things, Hamlet acts, as John Dover Wilson has pointed out, with an almost bewildering 'recklessness' throughout the play, giving most of his actions and decisions little thought whatsoever (Wilson, 92, 94, 141). What may seem a 'gap' in Hamlet's motivation, then, and why he seems not to know 'Why yet I live to say this thing's to do' (4.4.43) at various points, leaves him wide open to speculation: open, that is, to the kind of 'character criticism' that seeks to fill this gap and to explain Hamlet's 'delay' in ingenious but often extratextual ways – as the procrastination of Coleridge's contemplative man, or Bradley's melancholic prince, or Freud's Oedipal subject, and so on (see de Grazia 2007, 158–204).

Hamlet's soliloquies, then, may give us a distinct (but also a false, or at least incomplete) impression of what kind of play *Hamlet* finally is: one in which the drama of action appears to be substituted by a drama of character, at the centre of which stands Hamlet and his 'delay'. But we should hardly be surprised by this effect. For, as a dramatic device, the soliloquy seems designed to draw our attention to 'character', and especially to 'that within'. The primary importance of the soliloquy – why it remains 'one of the theatre's great potencies' (Pennington, 40) – lies in the way it appears to invite us into the interior or private space of a character, either by giving us the idea that we are overhearing thoughts and thought-processes (and being given access to hidden aspects of 'character' in that way), or because it establishes 'a form of dialogue' between a character and the play's spectators or readers, in which 'the speaker advances his understanding of himself and his complicity with them' (Pennington, 95, n.19). By breaking down the illusory 'fourth wall' of the stage and addressing us directly, we may feel drawn into a more direct engagement with a character – a sympathy, an understanding, a shared point of view – which would otherwise be missing, or at least much less intense. Great Shakespearean villains such as Iago and Richard III remain so dangerously attractive for just this reason, it seems, irrespective of their ethical or moral concerns. As with Hamlet, we are magnetized by them because they appear to confide in us alone, speaking to us as if openly and in an almost confessional way (see Hussey, 177–91; Palfrey, 221–47; Newell; Hirsh). But by allowing us to see and hear their ideas, schemes and plots in a way denied to other characters in the play, the information soliloquies provide also enhances our sense of dramatic irony and suspense – our sheer enjoyment of a play – significantly. In this sense, the soliloquy is such a powerful device not just because it encourages us to see the action of a play from a particular speaker's viewpoint or because it provides something like (but very different from) cinematic 'voiceover', but because it engages us in the very business of the play's action and plot: in the formation of character and irony.

Perhaps the greatest illusion the Shakespearean soliloquy effects, however, is that it can make a character seem *knowable*. By speaking to us both directly and also so regularly as a confessional and confiding subject – as a first-person speaker, a private 'I' – the soliloquies of *Hamlet* can give the impression of opening Hamlet's 'real' character to us. Because the soliloquy suddenly appears to make 'audible the personal voice' and to offer 'access to the presence of an individual speaker', then it has traditionally been seen, as Catherine Belsey (among others) has noted, as key to the way Shakespeare produces 'interiority effects' (Belsey, 42). Because a 'self-speaking' character such as Hamlet seems to offer himself as a coherent, unified presence on stage, a character who appears to know himself or at least to be able to reflect upon the 'self' in what seem to be open and telling ways, we might assume that soliloquies guarantee something about our understanding of that character (Hillman, 119–20). In Hamlet's case, the speaking of so many soliloquies in itself may doubly confirm an already pre-established expectation of character paralyzed by thinking. For not only do the soliloquies fix Hamlet before us on stage, pausing the plot to focus on what we might wish to consider his interior being or character, but by their very nature they seem to privilege the action of an interior life. As a result, they could easily serve to complete a circular argument about Hamlet's 'character', turning him into what we may already think he is: a protagonist of many words and many thoughts, but hardly a man of action.

But such assumptions about Hamlet's soliloquies are beset by many problems. Any instinctive sense we might have that soliloquies somehow guarantee access to an individual's inward 'presence' or to the true thoughts of a true self are complicated throughout *Hamlet* by the fact that Hamlet's acts of self-speaking rarely clarify or explain anything about his character. The more Hamlet speaks, in fact, the more uncertain we may become about why 'this thing's' still 'to do'. While the tendency for many critics has been to fill the incomplete 'character' of Hamlet's delay through inferred or assumed motivations (some of which are too deep psychologically even for Hamlet to recognize), for others, such as Catherine Belsey, the problem is equally clear. Although the speaker of a soliloquy (the 'subject of the enunciation') 'is there before us on the stage, palpably a unity', nevertheless what is said ('the subject of the utterance, the subject inscribed in the speech') can often seem 'fragmented' and 'discontinuous', especially in Hamlet's case. Because 'the "I" cannot be fully present in what it says of itself' in soliloquy, as Belsey puts it, then what emerges is a 'gap' between the speaker and the speaker's true 'subjectivity' ('that within'), and it is this 'gap' that 'opens the possibility of glimpsing an identity behind what is said', which it has been the 'project' of 'humanist criticism' to fill (Belsey, 46–9). Because Hamlet's soliloquies elude rather than confirm any final conclusions about his 'character', then our critical attention should 'focus on the subject of the utterance' (that is, what Hamlet is actually saying in any soliloquy, at any given point) rather than on 'the subject of the enunciation' (the speaker's elusive 'I': the 'self' supposedly hidden behind the words).

Hamlet's soliloquies cannot be trusted, in other words, to convey the kind of 'interiority' and access to 'character' that we might otherwise assume. We may instinctively consider the 'To be, or not to be' speech, for example, as deeply confessional and indeed 'characteristic', evolving (as we have already noted) as a profound meditation on matters that appear intrinsic to Hamlet's identity. It follows the thread of the opening lines of his first soliloquy in 1.2 (about 'self-slaughter'), and it continues to evoke a sense of world-weariness in Hamlet likewise established in that first soliloquy, before moving into considerations of 'conscience' and 'the name of action'. Moreover, this speech seems to invite a recognition of psychological depth in Hamlet, not just because he seems to be debating suicide, but because it offers a language of 'sleep' and of 'dreams' which 'Must give us pause' when considering his character (3.1.63–7). Freudian psychology reads us, after all, as the stuff that dreams are made on. In musing on how fearful it can be 'to dream', Hamlet seems to be touching on something profoundly human and personal here.

Or is he? As many commentators have noted, there is much in this speech to make us question how far we are entering Hamlet's mind. For of all Hamlet's soliloquies, 'To be, or not to be' is also the most impersonal: not once here does Hamlet speak of himself in the first person – as an 'I' – the effect of which is to de-personalize his words considerably. The speech reads more as a philosophical meditation, a serious and scholarly essay, than a confession, as it deals throughout with general ideas that are applied quite generally. It possesses a measure of rhetorical control and order noticeably lacking from the more spontaneous outbursts of his first two soliloquies, and is more like the public 'I know not seems' speech of 1.2 in this respect. We can see why the idea that Hamlet speaks this speech while 'poring upon a book' – as he does in the quite different First Quarto version of *Hamlet* (*Hamlet* 2006b, 1603 text, 7: 110) – might make sense. This speech seems to offer a different quality of interiority: more contemplative and more considered, being a rational debate rather than a personalized exclamation, as if Hamlet is responding not to the promptings of his heart, but to the words and ideas of a philo-sophical treatise.

Perhaps most important for us to note, though, is the fact that 'To be, or not to be' is not strictly a soliloquy at all: when Hamlet enters, Ophelia is already on stage, having been placed there to entrap him into saying something for Polonius and Claudius to overhear, who are likewise on stage, albeit concealed. The question for readers, audiences and directors of *Hamlet* at this point becomes crucially not one of character, first and foremost, but of staging. As has been long debated, the point at which we would have Hamlet entering 3.1 could determine what kind of soliloquy he subsequently speaks. Crucially, the two early printed versions of the play, on which our modern editions are based, offer quite different options here. If Hamlet enters *after* Claudius and Polonius have left to hide them-selves (which is what happens in the 1623 Folio version of *Hamlet*, for instance), then the 'To be, or not to be' speech may well be read as meditative, confessional, and 'characteristic', as Hamlet would presumably be oblivious to their presence. But if Hamlet enters before they leave the stage to conceal themselves (as the stage direc-tion indicates in the 1604/05 Second Quarto text, with Hamlet appearing before Polonius says to Claudius, 'I hear him coming – withdraw, my lord' (3.1.54)), then in performance Hamlet may well be shown as fully aware that some plot is afoot, having already spotted them beforehand. In which case, the 'To be, or not to be' speech may well be more strategic than confessional, spoken by a Hamlet fully aware that he is being watched and overheard, and whose words are generalized enough to remain more suggestive, evasive and obfuscatory than personal or conclusive. Is Hamlet addressing deeply intimate, existential questions of being and non-being in this speech, as a prelude to his own suicide? Or could the opening 'question' also be seen as a more political dilemma, with Hamlet appearing to consider whether 'To be, or not to be' Denmark's king? This is just how this soliloquy was to be rewritten for a later play, *The Jewes Tragedy* (1630) by John Heminge, in which a character (one Eleazer) debates whether 'to be or not to be' a 'Sovereign by unlawful means': 'I, there's the doubt', this rebel states, for 'where's my honour then?' (quoted in Conklin, 22–3). Is Hamlet's talk of 'resolution' and 'conscience' that of a man contemplating his own death, then, or of a prince deliberately deceiving his hearers, and giving them what they may both want and yet fear to hear: that is, a pretended dilemma over how Hamlet will achieve his political ambitions, and whether or not Claudius is 'to be or not to be'?

To read the soliloquy of 3.1 in this way is to be reminded that Hamlet's moments of 'self-speaking' are hardly extraneous to the action of the play, but deeply embedded within it, and often in complex ways. The 'To be, or not to be' soliloquy does not function solely or even primarily to provide access to 'character' or to fill-out the drama of *Hamlet* as one essentially concerned with Hamlet's state of mind. It uses a rhetoric of inwardness and 'conscience' – like the 'I know not seems' speech of 1.2 – as a means of protecting the 'self', by enabling Hamlet to evade surveillance and to elude discovery of 'that within'. As such, it is the political circumstance in which Hamlet finds himself from the very beginning that could be seen as forcing into being 'the construction of a private self' at such times, with Hamlet's obscure 'interiority' and depth – 'that within' – becoming 'a self-imposed privacy', a retreat from a court that is oppressively (perhaps tyrannically) watchful of this 'powerless prince' from the start (Burns, 141–2).

The fact that theatre and film directors have often moved the soliloquy of 3.1 elsewhere, treating it as a stand-alone speech in order to make it a less ambiguous vehicle for Hamlet's procrastinating character, seems illustrative of the fact that it otherwise remains a much more complex speech, and a more important moment of action, than we might otherwise consider. But recognizing that the soliloquies in *Hamlet* bear a dramatic function beyond illustrating Hamlet's 'character' alone can also be useful for other reasons. For example, in the absence of a Chorus from *Hamlet* – a device often used in Renaissance drama to comment on the action of a play and to signal changes of time and scene – the soliloquies serve crucially to punctuate events as they unfold, to reflect upon where the plot is going, and to keep Hamlet's revenge before us as an ongoing concern.[3] To borrow Ophelia's phrase, Hamlet himself is 'as good as a chorus' (3.2.238), dominating the drama as the combined hero and comedian, prologue and narrator of his own tragedy (Bruster and Weimann, 11–12). As such, the soliloquies can hardly be said to disable the dramatic action, but rather to enable it. When Hamlet speaks the words 'Now I am alone' at the end of 2.2, for instance, we enjoy not just the irony of this statement (for how alone can Hamlet be before a theatre audience?) but welcome the opportunity to return to Hamlet 'alone' again, after an exhausting display of 'antics'. Far from postponing the action of revenge, then, the soliloquy of 2.2 (the longest of the play) marks an essential move forward in its plotting, as Hamlet concludes to employ the travelling players he has just met in order to 'catch the conscience of the King' (2.2.540). Berating himself as 'pigeon-livered' and lacking in 'gall' (l. 512) for not yet having killed that 'bloody, bawdy villain' (l. 515) is no sign of 'self-deception, vacillation, and ineptitude' here. It is rhetoric, a process of thinking, 'intended to spur him on to activity' (Hardin, 234, 236). Much the same could be said of Hamlet's reflections in the soliloquy of 4.4, though (as we shall see) this speech presents other kinds of complexities for us to address.

It would be a mistake, then, to consider Hamlet's soliloquies as somehow separate from or counter to the play's main action, or as privileging character over plot. As Edward Burns puts it, not only do they 'tend to offer some explicit pointer to the progress of the plot' in *Hamlet*, but they are also typically inspired less by 'that within' in any case, as they are 'usually triggered by his perception of some other person' (Burns, 146–7): by the Ghost in 1.5, for example, the Player in 2.2, Claudius at prayer in 3.3, or Fortinbras preparing for war in 4.4. Because Hamlet's soliloquies are reactive rather than self-generated or isolated, standing as energized responses to the actions of others around him rather than simply as an expression of that permanently 'within', they cannot fix Hamlet's character beyond the moment at which they are spoken. Instead, they provide in-the-moment 'redefinitions of and by Hamlet, in the face of an audience' (Burns, 151, 147). Because they constitute no simplistic 'portrayal of moral choice and moral dilemma', Hamlet's soliloquies refuse to establish or confirm any 'static conception of who the Prince is' in the play. This is not to say that Hamlet's 'character' is essentially 'empty' or 'gestural' either. Rather, it is to see the soliloquies as providing key points in the dynamic development of Hamlet's character and its 'rhetorical action' (Burns, 151), rather than as fixed and deadening end points in 'character'. As such, the soliloquies mark the 'passage' rather than the 'essence' of Hamlet's 'character', as Michel de Montaigne might put it: each speech is a door opening onto his character as if afresh, rather than tagging it for purposes of identification, or enclosing it like a dramatic dead-end (Lee, 202).

If the soliloquies in *Hamlet* are 'moments of construing, moments in which the Prince attempts to reconstrue himself', then their 'rhetorical action' can be seen as 'above all the demonstration of the fluidity and processional nature of the Prince', who stands before us as 'an active, self-producing subject', and a figure 'constantly subject to change' (Lee, 179–84). They give us Hamlet's character both in and as a 'process of construction'. For this reason, Hamlet is rarely more dynamic or on the move as a character than in the action of his soliloquies, which remain the vehicles for an unfolding 'drama of thought' throughout *Hamlet* rather than expressions of a fixed kind of 'dramatized thinking' (Lee, 183). In soliloquy, we have the Hamlet who is ready to 'drink hot blood' at 3.2.380, and yet who refuses to kill Claudius in 3.3; who knows not why he lives 'to say this thing's to do' at 4.4.43, but even at this most hopeless point, implicitly recognizes that 'this thing's to do' while yet he lives.

DULL REVENGE

There are other aspects to the timeworn idea of Hamlet as a procrastinating hero to which we should also pay attention, and which concern questions of the substance or fabric of *Hamlet* itself, especially in terms of its textual variants (the differences between the early printed Quarto and Folio versions of the play, upon some of which we have touched already), and how these might reconstitute Hamlet's character and the quality of his revenge. For example, the soliloquy of 4.4 – which famously begins 'How all occasions do inform against me' (l. 31) – plays an important role in the construction of Hamlet's alleged delay not just because it brings to the fore the question of Hamlet's 'dull revenge' (4.4.32), but because it has an awkward textual status. Hamlet's final soliloquy appears in the Second Quarto version of *Hamlet* (published in 1604/05), but is notably absent from the later 1623 version of the play (collected in the large format Folio edition of Shakespeare's *Comedies, Histories, and Tragedies*, published seven years after his death). The two principal printed versions of the play, extant during and shortly after Shakespeare's lifetime, and upon which all modern editions of *Hamlet* are based, differ significantly, in other words, when it comes to the soliloquy of 4.4. In the earlier text, Hamlet gives this speech, and in the later one, he does not. This difference alone complicates our sense of when, why, and how often Hamlet seems to pause in his revenge. Unlike his 1604 twin, the 1623 Hamlet does not admit that 'I do not know / Why yet I live to say this thing's to do' at 4.4.42–3, because his last soliloquy in the play is the one he speaks when contemplating the murder of a praying Claudius in 3.3. Nor, then, does he confess his 'dull revenge', nor is he troubled by that 'delicate and tender prince', Fortinbras, whose amassing armies he sees only in the Second Quarto, and he certainly does not remind us that he may have been 'thinking too precisely on th'event' (4.4.40). By doing all of the above, the Hamlet of the Second Quarto may appear to delay in a way that the Folio Hamlet simply does not.

The first readers of *Hamlet*, those who bought the pocket-sized Quarto text of 1604/5 (advertised as 'Newly imprinted and enlarged [. . .] according to the true and perfect Coppie', to mark its authority, presumably, over the textually shorter and much more variable First Quarto *Hamlet*, published in 1603), would have been confronted not just by a *Hamlet* significantly different from the later Folio edition in numerous places: they likewise would have faced two slightly, but significantly, differing Hamlets. While this 'now-you-see-me, now-you-don't' quality of the 1604/05 and 1623 Hamlets seems fitting for a dramatic character who is always flickering before the gaze in *Hamlet*, leaving us never quite sure whether it is the real Prince or an alternative 'antic' version of himself we are watching or reading, nevertheless some of the implications this major textual difference presents for our reading of Hamlet's 'character' are obvious. Which is the 'real' or 'authentic' Hamlet? The one who speaks the soliloquy of 4.4, and seems doubly conscious of his 'delay', or the one who does not, and so is not? Which 'Hamlet' did Shakespeare intend for us to see?

Scholars and editors of *Hamlet* have long debated this textual puzzle. One line of thought is that the 1623 *Hamlet* (published in an edition that, like the Second Quarto, also advertised its contents as printed from the true and original copies of Shakespeare's plays), is a final version of the play revised by Shakespeare himself, in order to make more dramatic sense both of 4.4 and of the play as a whole. For, on the one hand, the 'How all occasions' soliloquy of 4.4 might be regarded as 'redundant' (as G.R. Hibbard, the editor of the Oxford Shakespeare *Hamlet* notes), because it seems largely to repeat the 'delay' soliloquy of 2.2. Cutting the speech would also give the actor playing Hamlet a much-needed break, Hibbard suggests, having been on stage 'almost continuously' since near the beginning of 2.2 (*Hamlet* 1987, 109). On the other hand, what Hamlet says in this speech does not make entire sense either. As the most recent Arden editors note, when Hamlet says 'I do not know / Why yet I live to say this thing's to do', given that he has 'strength and means / To do't', it is unclear how this can be so or why he even says this, 'as he is being escorted out of the country' at this point, on his way to England (*Hamlet* 2006a, 370, n.44). What 'strength', then? What 'means'?

On this basis, we might argue for the authority of the Folio version over the Second Quarto, and agree that 'cutting' the soliloquy of 4.4 may make sense, for a number of reasons. Whether Shakespeare made such a cut – whether it is a revision, or an authorial 'second thought' – is a separate question. Yet given the significance of the speech in other ways (its importance as a reflection on the empty heroism and 'honour' of armies ready 'to find quarrel in a straw', for instance, and in offering a key point of contrast between Hamlet and Fortinbras, not to mention its sheer quality as dramatic verse), we can see why editors have been reluctant to see it disappear from any modern edition of the play. More than anything, it keeps Hamlet's revenge in the frame of the action, and reminds us that the game is somehow still afoot. In this respect, the Second Quarto's soliloquy at 4.4 offers a crucial rhetorical counterpart to Hamlet's earlier admission to Gertrude in 3.4 (in a passage again found only in the 1604/05 Second Quarto text, and not in the Folio version) that, having somehow been made aware of a plot against him in being sent to England, he now plans to 'hoist' Rosencrantz and Guildenstern by their own 'petard' (3.4.200–8). One might argue to keep such passages from the Second Quarto in any edition of *Hamlet* precisely because they reveal a Hamlet whose ability to devise cunning plots and to keep his revenge alive make him much more a man of action in a way that he simply is not in the 1623 Folio text (in which Hamlet goes to England without comment, leaving us without any sense of what he is going to do next, or how he will make a comeback). When Hamlet leaves for England in the 1623 Folio version, the business of his revenge seems almost certainly to be over: in the 1604/05 text, it certainly is not.

The editorial tradition of conflating the 1604/05 and 1623 versions of *Hamlet* (whereby everything not included in one text is added to the other, allowing for a more 'complete' text of the play, as it were) does not solve the problem. Such a synthetic text of *Hamlet* not only bears a distorted resemblance to the originally printed Second Quarto or Folio texts, constituting a play that Shakespeare 'never wrote and which had never been acted' (John Jones, 127), but it also exacerbates the illusion of Hamlet's delay. In conflated versions,

Hamlet still speaks the soliloquy of 4.4 and all the other lines he has in the 1604/05 *Hamlet*, but he also speaks all of the lines given to him in the 1623 text. The gross result of such a cumulative version of the play (originally produced in 1733 by Lewis Theobald, arguably the first of Shakespeare's thorough and systematic modern editors (Walsh, 111–49)), is that it can skew our view of Hamlet as a character and as a hero significantly. By having more words to say than either of the 1604/05 or 1623 Hamlets, and by having not one but two soliloquies to speak about delay (in 2.2 and 4.4), the Hamlet of a conflated *Hamlet* may appear, all of a sudden, to take a lot longer over his revenge than ever before, and through the doubling of the soliloquies at 2.2 and 4.4, to procrastinate 'without any adequate reason being given' (John Jones, 131; see also Levin, 47).

For John Jones, who has argued stridently for the 1623 Folio *Hamlet* as the play that Shakespeare intended us finally to have, the 'conflating' tradition in which the play has been edited since Theobald's text of 1733 'goes to the heart of all judgement about delay', and so to the question of Hamlet's character (John Jones, 130). Because Romantic commentators of the late eighteenth and early nineteenth centuries, such as Coleridge and Hazlitt, were by that point reading an 'armchair' version of *Hamlet* that was really a merging of two related but separate earlier texts, and which exaggerated Hamlet's supposed 'delay' significantly, then a question naturally arose for them which had not, it seems, been asked before Theobald's cumulative edition appeared: why does Hamlet procrastinate so much? Hamlet's delay, in other words, and the eighteenth-century fascination for explaining it, may be due (in part, at least) to how editors have dealt with the different *Hamlet*s and their Hamlets, rather than to 'that within' the character of Hamlet himself. It might well be 'a feature of the editorial process of textual conflation and accretion as much as of the dramatist's original design' (Jardine 1996, 155).[4]

In offering this argument, Jones wishes for readers of *Hamlet* 'to unthink an entire critical tradition' (John Jones, 130). Our aim, however, can remain more modest. What the textual history of *Hamlet* reminds us is simply that we should be wary of assuming that a 'character' like Hamlet is fixed as an unchanging identity, or is in possession of an 'essence' that is permanent, if only because different versions of *Hamlet* give us different Hamlets (however slight). Character is not something, then, that stands apart from or in any sense transcends what might seem mundane matters of textual history or the decisions of editors and stage or film directors, who likewise adapt the texts of *Hamlet* and in the process create or reveal potentially very distinct Hamlets. Rather, character is dependent and contingent upon them. To this extent, it would be more accurate to say that every Hamlet edited or performed, on the stage or on the page, is a different – though related – 'character', with a distinct quality and sense of 'self', albeit one produced and conducted within a continuum of editorial and theatrical traditions (see especially *Hamlet* 1999, and Holmes). Olivier's 1948 film adaptation appears to give us a very particular Hamlet from the outset by cutting, as we saw in the last chapter, the Prince's crucial opening two lines in 1.2; whereas in the eighteenth century David Garrick, the great Shakespearean actor-manager, decided more audaciously to cut from *Hamlet* the entire business of Act 5 (all those gravediggers and fight scenes), which he regarded as pure 'rubbish' (Dawson, 40–3). Hamlet's 'character', then, from its first printing to its continued adaptation in screen and stage performance, should be considered less an immoveable entity and more of a moveable feast: like the play, it is a machine of moving but also of removable and interchangeable parts.

HAMLET AND AMLETH

Another factor to bear in mind when it comes to reading Hamlet's character as a revenger concerns the play's historical analogues and sources. Although the most immediate and likely source for Shakespeare's *Hamlet* is no longer extant (an earlier revenge tragedy of the same title, possibly written by Thomas Kyd, author of *The Spanish Tragedy*, to which Shakespeare's *Hamlet* also bears numerous affinities), and while there is no evidence that Shakespeare would have known the story of Hamlet from anywhere else, nevertheless seeing how Shakespeare's play both compares to and differs from the old legend of Amleth can be useful when it comes to reviewing Hamlet's character as a revenge hero. There are two earlier versions of the story of Amleth, in fact: the 'Life' of Hamlet or Amleth included in the Latin *Gesta Danorum* or *History of the Danes*, composed by Saxo Grammaticus around 1200, first printed in the early sixteenth century; and the translation of this story into French (with slight alterations) by François de Belleforest in the fifth volume of *Histoires Tragiques*, published in 1570. The Hamlets of these accounts are far from inadequate heroes, reluctant revengers, or characters of procrastination. Rather, as is summarized at one point in Saxo's account, the original Amleth is legendary for his unambiguous heroism: 'A brave man and deserving to be remembered! He shrewdly played the fool' and through 'his cunning he saved not only his own life but also managed to avenge his father', becoming victorious over his murderous stepfather (one Feng, Fengi, or Fengon) through great 'courage' and 'cleverness' (Hansen, 107). One notable difference from Shakespeare's Hamlet in this respect is obvious: the Amleth of Danish legend manages to take his vengeance not just ruthlessly and heroically, but successfully, going on to become king himself and to prosper.

Many of the key elements in Shakespeare's story of Hamlet are certainly to be found in these legendary accounts: Amleth vows to avenge his father's murder, committed by an uncle who also marries Amleth's mother (Geruth or Gerutha), and – avoiding various traps laid for him – he plays the fool in order to appear politically harmless and to buy time to devise a worthy plan of revenge. In this sense, the most notable point of continuity between Shakespeare's Hamlet and the Amleth of these accounts lies, ironically, in delaying vengeance. As William F. Hansen points out: 'No Hamlet [that is, neither Saxo's nor Belleforests's nor Shakespeare's] attempts revenge immediately upon his learning of the murder of his father: all Hamlets delay' (Hansen, 74–5). This point reminds us of Peter Mercer's argument about how pausing for thought is essential to the action of revenge. But there are some crucial differences to note between Saxo's and Belleforest's Amleths and Shakespeare's Hamlet when it comes to delay. In the earlier narrative accounts, the 'delay' is forced upon Amleth by 'obstacles' that are 'completely external in nature': Amleth is a mere 'youth' who is 'pitted against a powerful and villainous king', and so he has to wait, in order to mature and to devise the best way of killing his uncle in a way that would be justifiable to his people, while also preserving his own life and evading suspicion in the meantime (Hansen, 75). The result is a story of revenge patiently awaited, carefully planned and ruthlessly executed, without any question of unsuitability or reluctance or conflicted motivation. Without this particular set of 'external obstacles', Shakespeare's Hamlet appears to face 'internal' problems – usually accounted for via psychology or 'character', as we have seen – which result in a revenge that has traditionally been regarded as postponed rather than planned, and which is taken at the very end more by accident, it might seem, than by design.

Yet perhaps the greatest difference between Shakespeare's story of Hamlet's revenge and the earlier accounts of Amleth, the single factor that explains why revenge is more problematic in *Hamlet*, is simpler still. Whereas in Saxo's and Belleforest's accounts, the murder of Amleth's father (here known as Horwendil or Ørvendil) is public knowledge from the start – it is a villainous crime of which everyone is aware, but which Fengi 'disguised' and justified 'as an act of duty' in order to become king (Hansen, 97) – in Shakespeare's play the murder of which Claudius is guilty is not publicly known. It seems to be known by no one except Claudius himself (and only in the prayer scene of 3.3 do we, as readers and spectators, finally hear a full and unambiguous confession of the murder, at last confirming his 'offence' once and for all). The murder in Shakespeare's plot is, then, committed in private, and knowledge of it remains a secret throughout the play: it is never made public at all, in fact. Much more than the idea that Shakespeare's Hamlet is a Renaissance Christian prince caught in a pagan story of revenge otherwise determined by Nordic heroic codes and values (which is another way of explaining Hamlet's alleged 'dilemma'), the fact that old Hamlet's murder was done in secret has by far the greatest effect on the character of Hamlet's revenge. For if the original crime is a secret, then presumably it must first be made public for any act of revenge to be justified, one might think. What kind of revenge could Hamlet take against Claudius 'without convicting him publicly' in the process (Hansen, 75)? This issue still remains a problem at the very end of the play. At the point at which Hamlet does eventually murder Claudius in 5.2 (around l. 309), it appears to the other characters remaining on stage (other than Horatio, that is) as an act of sudden and unjustifiable 'treason, treason' (as they cry out), for both Claudius's murder of old Hamlet and his plot to kill young Hamlet are still unknown to everyone else.

But there are more important consequences of the murder taking place in secret. On one level, we can see that by turning the murder of old Hamlet into a private crime, Shakespeare is granted an obvious dramatic opportunity: he can have news of this heinous act erupt spectacularly in the play through supernatural means, in the form of *Hamlet*'s ghoulish messenger, the Ghost. Without the Ghost, how else would Hamlet (or any of us) know that old Hamlet had died of anything other than natural causes? The Ghost is crucial, then, in making known that murder has taken place, and that it requires vengeance. Because in Saxo's and Belleforest's accounts the murder is in the public realm, naturally there is no need for such spiritual intervention. The presence of the Ghost in Shakespeare's *Hamlet* may well be a throwback to the earlier (but now lost) version of *Hamlet* (often referred to as the *Ur-Hamlet*), about which we know very little other than that it had a Ghost which (like Shakespeare's) bellowed out its commands for 'revenge' (albeit 'like an oyster-wife', according to Thomas Lodge) (*Hamlet* 2006a, 44–7). But having the Ghost become the messenger of the play's crime, and the source of the revenge, is problematic on another level: standing as both the victim and the only witness to the murder committed by Claudius, is the Ghost to be trusted? As the only 'proof' that any crime has taken place, in fact, the Ghost offers itself to Hamlet as a deeply problematic body of evidence with which to prosecute Claudius, primarily because it is no body at all.

For this reason, both the secrecy of the murder and the means by which it is revealed to Hamlet leave him and the business of his revenge in a state of epistemological uncertainty notably absent from the Amleth legend. Is the only source of information about the murder in Shakespeare's *Hamlet* reliable? How can we know? Given that Hamlet's initial action as a revenger is to swear Marcellus and Horatio to further secrecy, it seems that part of the difficulty Hamlet faces is both how to make his cause public, and how to know whether the Ghost is telling the truth or not. Such are the uncertainties Hamlet articulates in the 'rogue and peasant' soliloquy of 2.2, of course, in which he expresses no doubt about wanting to take revenge, and frustration at being left 'unpregnant of my cause' (2.2.503): not just powerless to act, that is, but able to 'say nothing' to further his 'cause' other than to 'fall a-cursing' impotently, 'like a very drab' (l. 521). The doubts that Hamlet subsequently expresses in this soliloquy about the ambivalent nature of the Ghost – whether it is in fact a devil trying to 'damn' him (ll. 533–8) – are far from an afterthought or a paltry excuse to delay or a sign of a psychological flaw ('that within') preventing him from taking action. It is, rather, a mark of how the complications in Hamlet's revenge are 'logically connected to and to some extent follow from the secrecy of the initial murder' (Hansen, 76). What follows the soliloquy of 2.2 in *Hamlet* – the play-within-the play of 3.2, and all that follows that in turn – stems directly from this key issue: the secrecy of old Hamlet's murder, and how young Hamlet must find 'grounds / More relative' (2.2.538–9) than the Ghost's story alone as the basis for his revenge.

All of this has very particular effects upon the quality of Hamlet's revenge, and upon our view of Hamlet as a character of revenge. While the question of a murder undertaken in secret naturally gives Hamlet (and us) cause to pause for thought, the fact that the burden of proof in the play rests on the appearance of a deeply ambivalent Ghost of 'questionable shape', and which could be either 'wicked or charitable' (1.4.41–3) also establishes an unsettling double perspective upon the play and upon Hamlet's actions. Not only are we unsure about who may or may not be complicit in Claudius's crime (Gertrude and Polonius, for instance?), but from our privileged position as spectators or readers, we can also see the action unfolding from both Hamlet's and other characters' perspectives simultaneously. What gives Hamlet all the proof he requires to convict Claudius of murder – that is, Claudius's reaction to *The Mousetrap* performed in 3.2 – on the contrary provides no proof at all to anyone else: even Horatio seems less than convinced that the conscience of the King has been caught by this play-within-the-play. Given that *The Mousetrap* is a play that depicts a nephew (Lucianus) murdering his uncle (Gonzago), how else would we (or any other onstage characters) expect Claudius to react to this business? What we are watching with Hamlet in 3.2 is, as a result, quite different from what the other characters might be seeing. Because *The Mousetrap* confirms the suspicions of both Claudius and Hamlet at the same time, with the King now 'convinced that Hamlet may try to kill him' and with Hamlet equally 'convinced that Claudius killed his father' (Hansen, 77), we see this moment as if in double vision. The same effect is achieved in 5.2 when Hamlet kills Claudius. This final act of revenge can make sense to no one else left on stage, with the exception of Horatio, who is left to tell the tale at the end. Hamlet's final act of heroism before dying, the climax of his revenge, can only appear unmotivated – mad, even – to the surviving courtiers of Elsinore. How does Hamlet's revenge really end, then? Not with a bang, but a whimper?

TO PLAY THE FOOL

The fact that the murder is kept secret in *Hamlet* also makes Hamlet's decision to adopt an 'antic disposition' – to play the fool in a way dictated by the legendary story and by the name Amleth itself, as a variation on an Old Norse word meaning 'stupid' – appear strangely unmotivated. Whereas the Amleth in Saxo and Belleforest pretend to be mad in order to avoid being murdered as a potential claimant to the throne, and to evade suspicion in taking revenge, Shakespeare's Hamlet has no need to do so. As only Claudius knows of the murder of Hamlet's father, Hamlet's 'antic disposition' seems to work entirely counterproductively. It is only Hamlet's extrovert fooling and his displays of 'madness' that draw Claudius's attention to him from Act 2 onwards, and which instinctively arouse the King's suspicions. Hamlet's antic disguise, in other words, fools Claudius not for one minute: he knows from the outset that something is up.

Although we can see how Hamlet's pretended madness and foolery help to disguise his motivations in a chaotic show of misdirection and evasion, and while we might be tempted also to conclude that this 'antic disposition' permits him to delay his revenge in a time-honoured fashion (creating further room for the kinds of psychological explanation of his character that developed from the eighteenth century onwards, as Margreta de Grazia has shown (2007, 158–204)), nevertheless his performance as the play's fool highlights an important aspect of his own construction as a genre-defying character, and one that Hamlet himself draws our attention to in his famous 'advice to the players' speech of 3.2.1–43. When directing his final instructions to the visiting company's 'clowns', insisting that they 'speak no more than is set down for them' (l. 37), Hamlet seems to know full well that comedians will always be tempted to 'set on some quantity of barren spectators to laugh too' (l. 39) – to improvise and go 'off-script', that is, and so to step out of character for the sake of an easy guffaw from the audience – 'though in the meantime some necessary question of the play be then to be considered' (ll. 40–1). To lose the name of the play's action – to lose the plot – for the sake of a quick gag is 'villainous' (l. 41), Hamlet concludes. Yet, ironically, this is an accurate way of regarding Hamlet's own decision to adopt the persona of a clown – an 'antic disposition' – in the play. What else is Hamlet other than a character who seems continually to go 'off script', and to 'speak more' than is 'set down' for him in any of his otherwise fixed roles and identities: as prince, courtier, scholar, son, lover, avenger? And what is Hamlet's 'antic disposition' in the play other than as a marker quite literally of his role as revenger: as 'villainous' clown, improvising his revenge in deadly play?

Hamlet's language here serves to remind us of just how complicated the character of Hamlet's revenge can be to unravel, and of just how much is involved in the construction of Hamlet's character as an avenging hero-villain-clown. Yet it also offers a point of contrast for us to note when, having escaped death on his way to England, Hamlet returns to Denmark via the graveyard of 5.1, to banter with those other villainous clowns, the gravediggers, and to meditate on the skull of Yorick, the court jester whose role Hamlet has usurped in *Hamlet* up to this point. Through the introduction of these professional fools, we can sense a major shift in Hamlet's sensibilities as a revenger as the play draws towards its close. What is distinctly noticeable about the Hamlet who returns from sea at this point is that as a character of revenge, he seems to have undergone a sea change. Not only has he put off his 'antic disposition' – presenting himself to the courtly mourners attending Ophelia's funeral strictly as himself, and famously pronouncing himself as 'I, / Hamlet the Dane' (5.1.246–7) – but on returning from his journey, quite conspicuously, he no longer speaks in soliloquy. The key markers of his identity as a revenger – the Ghost, the soliloquy and his antic disposition – are effectively dropped from his part in Act 5.

What takes their place is a very different quality of revenge: one that is determined both by the plot against Hamlet by Claudius and Laertes to avenge the murder of Polonius (crucially turning Hamlet into a victim rather than a prosecutor of revenge in Act 5), and by a rhetoric of a fateful resignation to 'providence' (Mercer, 226–49). With proof in hand of Claudius's attempt to murder Hamlet – this, rather than his father's murder, now being central to Hamlet's cause and his 'perfect conscience' (5.2.66) – the Hamlet of Act 5 appears brilliantly to have been transformed from an antic revenger into a stoical victim, who resigns his will to the providence of God and who accepts a challenge to a swordfight that Horatio knows he cannot win. It is in this change in the character of Hamlet's revenge that Hamlet's final transformation is effected. In killing Claudius, and in dying himself, Hamlet becomes – quite impossibly – both the Ghost's 'apt' revenger and Horatio's 'sweet Prince': at last, he is the play's revenge hero and its tragic victim.

CHAPTER 3

FAMILIES, FRIENDS, ENEMIES: *HAMLET*'S OTHER CHARACTERS

'It may be properly said of this play', wrote Anthony Ashley Cooper, third Earl of Shaftesbury in *Characteristics of Men, Manners, Opinions, Times* (2nd edn 1714), 'that it has only one character or principal part', being 'a series of deep reflections drawn from one mouth' in 'almost one continued moral'. It is through this singular quality that *Hamlet* 'appears to have most affected English hearts, and has perhaps been oftenest acted of any which have come upon our stage' (Cooper, 124). Three centuries on, it seems difficult to refute such a view. Given that Hamlet both speaks the most lines and performs the most soliloquies, and so remains on stage longer than any other character, and given also that Hamlet's part constitutes what seems like a whole cast of roles (from revenge hero to comedian, from madman and lover to tragic prince), we may well consider *Hamlet* to be something of a one-man show. We may even think of *Hamlet* as a drama that has been constructed through or around the consciousness of its hero, as if its action is somehow taking place within and without Hamlet's own mind.

Curiously, the presence of other characters in *Hamlet* does not detract from this effect. Even on those occasions when Hamlet is not on stage, he remains throughout almost exclusively the subject of others' conversations and speculations. As a result Hamlet is always at the very centre of *Hamlet*. Moreover, the play's other characters appear readily (perhaps too readily) to provide us with other versions of Hamlet, against which his character can be compared and contrasted continually. It is as if the play centres its hero in a labyrinth constructed of dramatic mirrors, at each turn of which we perceive a reflection of Hamlet himself, whether it is in Claudius as Hamlet's political (or even Oedipal) counterpart, or in Laertes as

Hamlet's opposite number, both in loving Ophelia and avenging a murdered father; in the warlike 'young Fortinbras', who gains the Danish crown in Hamlet's tragedy, or in the restless Ghost of 'old Hamlet' who lost the throne by 'foul play'; in his rational fellow student Horatio, or in the irrational Ophelia; in the Player of 2.2, or in the dead jester Yorick, resurrected in 5.1.

For Francis Barker, the fact that the play mobilizes so many 'simulacra' of Hamlet serves to highlight how Hamlet's 'interiority' and his status as an 'essential' being are denied by the text, which 'disperses across its surface [. . .] other, external versions of the prince, in order to fend off the insistence of his unique essentiality'(Barker, 35). For Bert O. States, however, the way in which *Hamlet*'s other characters 'perform as satellite figures who reflect and draw out the energies of the solar figure from whom they receive their individual life' works less to empty Hamlet of subjectivity than it does to give *them* 'the impression of depth', as they both 'iterate' and are iterated by Hamlet's character in turn (Barker, 89). Viewing *Hamlet* in such ways permits us to see that 'the self that is dramatized' in it can be seen as 'more an ensemble of possible selves than a study of a single consciousness plagued with a determinable "problem" '. Yet the dramatic effect appears to be the same as that noted by Shaftesbury 300 years ago. *Hamlet* becomes 'a monologue, a drama of the "single figure" ' in these terms, the secondary characters of which seem largely to fulfil the role of 'illustrating the character of Hamlet', as if they are no more than 'dreamed [. . .] self-projections' or 'repetitions' of Hamlet himself (States, 90–2; Barker, 35).

The aim of this chapter is to examine the play's other characters not just as 'satellites' that orbit the hero and reflect a borrowed light, but as dramatic creations deserving critical illumination in their own right. How they function in the play, contributing to the action as highly individuated figures, each with a quite distinct dramatic role, will be our focus. By looking at the play's secondary characters, no matter how briefly (as must be the case here), we can see how questions that have traditionally been directed largely towards the character of Hamlet can also be crucial for reading *Hamlet*'s other parts. It is not just the Prince, for example, who appears to be radically 'discontinuous' (Belsey, 42), or who alone seems to suffer from neoclassical or psychological inconsistency when it comes to decorum and motivation. Much the same could be said of *Hamlet*'s other courtly fool, Polonius. Nor is it just the Prince who invites us to read the play through a 'penumbra of inferences' (Nuttall 2007, 176), as the kinds of questions that plague us about Hamlet often find their origins or their endpoints in the indeterminate actions and motivations of the other characters, and which subsequently invite suspicion about who has done what, when and why. Does Ophelia commit suicide, for example? Why does Polonius spy upon his own son? Whose side is Gertrude – or Horatio, for that matter – really on? An entire chapter – if not a whole book – could be dedicated to each of the play's secondary characters based upon the kinds of speculation they invite.

That the play's overall atmosphere of distrust and paranoia is enhanced powerfully by the doubts and uncertainties that hang over *Hamlet*'s other on-stage persons is without question. But what makes *Hamlet* inexhaustibly fascinating, and what imbues it with dramatic longevity, is not just that it focuses upon a single character, as Shaftesbury supposed, but that it places Hamlet within a dense matrix of characters all of whom have conflicting identities. It is as if *Hamlet* is a situation tragedy, in which familial and political roles become painfully tangled, leaving difficult matters of state to become inseparable from desperate states of mind. It is the secondary characters of *Hamlet*, much more than the Prince himself perhaps, who as a result defy dramatic categorization. They effectively make a mockery of how their roles are often presented in the kinds of *Dramatis Personae* imposed upon the play by editors keen to fix their identities as 'unitary' figures well in advance of us actually seeing or hearing them. Gertrude, for instance, resists summary in the style of any 'List of Characters' because her identity spills across the kinds of decorum and consistency that would otherwise confine her. She is the play's Queen and 'imperial jointress' (1.2.9), but her public and political function as such is complicated by her domestic and familial role as Hamlet's mother (or is she now technically his aunt?), as well as the old king's widow and the new king's bride, and so by the conflicting duties and loyalties she owes to each. As Hamlet bitterly reminds her in 3.4, she is 'the Queen', but also a 'husband's brother's wife, / And, would it were not so, my mother' (3.4.14–15). Gertrude is even given alternative speech prefixes in the early printed versions of the play: in 3.4, the harrowing 'closet scene', the 1623 Folio identifies her by her usual speech prefix '*Queene*' (which may signal her identity, even when alone with Hamlet, as politically determined, formal, official, stately), whereas the 1604/05 Second Quarto text abandons this typical speech prefix at this point in order to introduce her in 3.4 as '*Gertrard*' (indicating a different persona, potentially – more personal and intimate – as well as a change of costume, possibly). To ask who and what Gertrude is (Queen or mother, wife or widow) thus becomes as central to our experience of *Hamlet* as any uncertainty over the Prince himself.

We can see too why the play has been mined so often and for long as a psychological casebook. In *Hamlet*, Shakespeare deals implicitly and explicitly with the stuff of social and political changes as well as of mental and emotional charges, at the centre of which stand the dual businesses of state and of family, with the action drawing on the difficulties of familial bonds and relationships at almost every turn. Through this double lens, the politics of regicide (the killing of kings) becomes inseparable from the gruesomeness of parricide and fratricide (the murder of fathers and brothers), while marriage and motherhood likewise become tainted by implications of incest and illicit sexuality, ambition and guilt. It is hardly surprising that *Hamlet* would become so important in Freudian and Lacanian psychology, for Shakespeare's ability to corner the dark materials of the psyche is a prime source of *Hamlet*'s theatrical endurance and of its dramatic and emotional density, as well as of its political and psychological insightfulness. In the midst of a tragedy that negotiates the heady business of murder and of ghosts, of incest and of madness, of suicide and tyranny, Shakespeare centres dramatic attention on the fraught nature of families: on fathers and sons, brothers and sisters, husbands and wives, mothers and sons, fathers and daughters. Although Hamlet stands at the heart of all of this intense complexity, nevertheless the roots of these complications can hardly be said to lie in him alone. They reside, rather, in the play's other characters. It is their knots and their knottiness that we, like Hamlet, are left to untie.

KING, CLAUDIUS

After the Prince, the King is arguably the most important character in *Hamlet*: he has the second largest part in the play, and he appears on stage more often than any other secondary character. Only Claudius can rival Hamlet in his use of soliloquy, astonishing us with confessions of a tender conscience in the 'prayer scene' of 3.3, and with proof of his unredeemable villainy (again in soliloquy) at 4.3.56–66. His prominence is hardly surprising given that Claudius is, hierarchically, the most significant figure, but also that *Hamlet* is largely a play about two men plotting to kill one another, each for the most part unbeknownst to the other. As Hamlet's political and familial nemesis, then, and especially as his father's murderer, Claudius's role is central to a drama which, in many ways, works as a two-hander, with Hamlet and his uncle circling one another suspiciously throughout, and with their fortunes pivoting upon the same axes of action and accident. The murder of Polonius, for instance, sees Hamlet's role as a plotting revenger recede, by sealing his already confirmed exile to England at the end of Act 4, just as it forces Claudius to plot more intensely to murder Hamlet – to play the villain more openly – from this point on. In this way, *Hamlet* can be seen as a finely counterbalanced drama shared primarily between the Prince and the King, the son and the uncle, the murderer and the avenger.

But while the play invites such an easily schematized view, Claudius is a more complex character than just Hamlet's arch-enemy, and his identity is as precarious as anyone else's in *Hamlet*. Like Gertrude, he occupies various subject positions simultaneously, and this likewise makes it impossible to summarize his 'character' in the style of a *Dramatis Personae*: he is the King, but only because he is also a murderer, and he is a husband and a step-father for the same reason. How should Claudius's part be characterized, then? As rightful ruler or tyrant; a murderer or a loving husband? In this respect, how Claudius is identified by speech prefixes seems telling. If we have a modern edition of *Hamlet* in which his part is prefaced by the name '*Claudius*', then we are perhaps given a false sense of a nameable personality – someone known to us on first-name terms – despite the fact that he is never addressed as such in the play (not even by his wife). While in the early Quarto and Folio editions, he is described in a stage direction as entering 1.2 as '*Claudius King of Denmark*', nevertheless he only ever speaks as '*King*' in these texts. Why, then, would we first-name him as '*Claudius*' at all? We might do so because referring to him simply as the play's '*King*' can seem just as problematic. Because we may never be sure who the legitimate king is in *Hamlet*, then whether it is ever appropriate to refer to Claudius as such becomes difficult to say (see Stallybrass). Given that 'old Hamlet' was (and would still have been) the king had it not been for his murderous brother, and given also any initial disorientation we may experience at 'young Hamlet' not inheriting his father's throne, what right has Claudius to this title, we might wonder? In what sense is he actually 'king'? Yet marking Claudius's part as King can also help to underscore a crucial political difficulty Hamlet faces in taking his revenge. This title makes clear that it is not just his father's murderer Hamlet must kill, or his mother's husband, but his monarch: one properly elected, and – more critically – one appointed by God (as Claudius reminds Gertrude in 4.5.122–5).

Another problem we face when reading Claudius's character is that it can be tempting to regard him largely from Hamlet's point of view, particularly if we already know the story. As soon as he enters in 1.2, we may automatically identify Claudius as the villain of the play, whether we have any evidence for it or not, and see in him everything that we would expect of a man who has murdered his brother, and who is wearing a crown soaked in blood. When viewed from a perspective of prior knowledge about the crime that Claudius has committed (like an open secret, known to the audience, but not to other characters in the play), Claudius's opening speech in 1.2, in its greasy ability to yoke together weddings and funerals, mirth and mourning, can only confirm the hypocrisy of a villain who is capitalizing on his own treachery, and flaunting his new-found power through a rhetoric characterized by oxymoron and antithesis, as if by force of will he can make the unnatural appear natural, the abnormal normal. He is, as Stephen Booth describes him, 'the unifier of contraries' (Booth, 149). We may be tempted to go further, and see Claudius not as any king at all, but as a usurper and a tyrant, and thus to read backwards onto his language and behaviour all the traits with which Hamlet subsequently identifies him: villainous, lecherous, adulterous, murderous. Claudius's fundamental lack of moral fibre and his gluttony for power could also be signalled, especially in the absence of other telling signs of culpability, by an actor deciding to play the part slightly drunk. By picking up on Claudius's propensity to feast and revel in the play, and to which Hamlet objects, again quite puritanically, as a 'defect' and a 'vicious mole of nature', not just in his uncle but among most Danes (see 1.4.8–38), then a drunken Claudius, belching forth his paradox-ridden first speech, could easily become shorthand for the villain Hamlet (and perhaps the audience) wants him to be: a wicked tyrant, a filthy bawd, an ogre, an oaf.

Yet the King of 1.2 is none of these things. Because the first admission of Claudius's guilt appears only much later in the play (as an aside at 3.1.48–53, before we hear the full confession in soliloquy at 3.3.36–72), then we view both Hamlet and Claudius at the start of the play once again through a curious double perspective, seeing simultaneously what is and is not. For (as we explored in Chapter 1) if we had no prior knowledge of the story of *Hamlet*, we might well assume a reversal of roles in 1.2, with the new king appearing as the central character, and the silent man in black, his nephew, occupying the role of villain. But knowing about the murder (something hinted at by the Ghost's presence in 1.1, perhaps, yet in no sense communicated definitively), we see these polarities reversed, as we wait for signs of Claudius's villainy to emerge. The problem, though, is that it can be difficult to find any evidence of Claudius as a murderer before the prayer scene of 3.3, and this leaves the play without 'a clear centre of malevolence' (States, 99), and the audience in a state of uncertainty when it comes to reading his character. For, as G. Wilson Knight has famously pointed out, Claudius first appears in the play, contrary to our expectations, as something other than 'a criminal': he is, quite plausibly, 'a good and gentle king', who while preparing for war against Norway (as Horatio informs us in 1.1) is nevertheless shown in 1.2 prioritizing diplomacy over belligerence as a way of averting international conflict. Dispatching ambassadors for this purpose is the first and decisive action we see Claudius taking, and this alone marks his style of government as more subtle and sophisticated (and more modern, perhaps) than that of the former king (who achieved success more heroically – but perhaps more barbarically – by defeating old Fortinbras in combat). It is Hamlet, then, who seems to represent 'a danger to the state' in 1.2, rather than this administratively capable, smooth-tongued, happily married king (Knight, 33–8).

G. Wilson Knight no doubt overstates his case in reading Claudius, at the beginning of *Hamlet* at least, as 'the typical kindly uncle' and 'a goodly king' (Knight, 35): as we shall see, Claudius might be rather less than either in 1.2. Yet Wilson Knight's argument is useful in reminding us that it is all too easy to read Claudius simply as a 'type' rather than as a character whose identity shifts as the play progresses, albeit becoming increasingly fixed into the role of stage villain from 3.3 onwards: it is as if his inability to repent at this point hardens him irredeemably into a stereotypical 'character'. Such is

Claudius's tragedy, perhaps. It is easy to forget, moreover, that we are continually engaged by Shakespeare to see the action of *Hamlet* from both Hamlet's and his uncle's perspectives. While the story of the former is how to catch the conscience of a king who should not be king, and then to kill him, the story of the latter is how to keep an ill-gotten but hard-won crown from a nephew of whom he is deeply suspicious, and whose mysterious 'transformation' (2.2.5) he mistrusts implicitly. We are reminded repeatedly of the world that Claudius inhabits (one characterized by quiet panic, frustration and paranoia) by the number of times Shakespeare brings the King onto the stage reiterating the same desire to fathom Hamlet's 'drift' (doing so at the beginning of 2.2, again in 3.1, and again in 3.3, and yet again in 4.1). It is as if Claudius is caught in a nightmare of repetition when it comes to reading Hamlet's actions, the illegibility of Hamlet's character remaining for the King no curious conundrum, but a matter of life and death.

There is, however, much in 1.2 that signals Claudius's character beyond the idea that he is either Knight's 'kindly uncle' and 'goodly king', or the drunken, loutish tyrant of Hamlet's (or of our own) imagination. For a start, the rhetoric of Claudius's speeches in 1.2 defies any sense of drunken incoherence: it is simply too controlled and too effective to be uttered by a sot. Claudius's verbal poise also reveals him to be something quite other than an innocent, avuncular king. We have already considered (in Chapter 1) how Claudius's opening words – 'Of Hamlet' – serve simultaneously to place the Prince at the centre of the scene and to banish him to its margins, as the King goes on to address 'Hamlet our dear brother's death' as the proper subject of his opening oratory. For anyone aware that he has murdered his brother, this speech can be nothing but a studied work of hypocrisy, which seeks to smooth over the awkwardness of his (incestuous) marriage (so soon after the former king's funeral) in three ways: by effacing it through a balanced language of antithesis and oxymoron, as if the difficult decision to marry has been measured and weighed very carefully; by confirming the approval of this decision by the 'better wisdoms' of the court and council; and by beginning it all with a tender declaration of 'memory' and 'remembrance' when it comes to the former king-brother-husband (see 1.2.1–16). Claudius is careful not to overplay this rhetorical role: he puts an end to the difficult business of addressing this royal funeral-cum-marriage, and of balancing 'dole' with 'delight', in a simple and conclusive phrase: 'For all, our thanks' (1.2.16). He does not want to dwell on his dead brother too long, and besides he now has more important business to attend as king: war, diplomacy and other matters of state. His is a very slick opening performance.

Where Claudius comes unstuck is in turning his attention to Hamlet, upon whom the rhetoric that turns 'dole' (sorrow or sadness) into 'delight' simply does not work. Claudius attempts to gloss over Hamlet's uncomfortable and uncertain political position – and his new familial identity – by addressing him smoothly as both 'my cousin Hamlet, and my son' (1.2.64). But Hamlet takes immediate exception to these words, and he refuses outright to accept them. In doing so, the Prince comes dangerously close to exposing Claudius's careful binaries – of 'dole' and 'delight', 'mirth' and 'dirge', 'sister' and 'wife', 'cousin' and 'son' – as empty and fraudulent before the court. As we have already seen, by replying with the riddling (and also mockingly well-balanced) 'more than kin, and less than kind' (1.2.65), Hamlet reveals that he is far from under the sway of Claudius's politic pose: he draws attention to the very things the new king would rather bury than remember. In marrying his brother's wife, and his 'sometime sister', Hamlet's cutting replies to this king about being too much in the 'son' and being more than 'kin' and less than 'kind' (more than 'cousin' now, but certainly less than Claudius's natural son, bearing no resemblance to him in 'kind' at all) seem designed to highlight the uncomfortably incestuous implications of his mother's remarriage, and thus to undermine the entire moral basis of the new regime. Hamlet's first two lines work effectively, then, to dismantle the opening 16 lines of Claudius's speech in 1.2 in two quick-witted passes of his sharp tongue. Does the Queen intervene so quickly at this point with her 'Good Hamlet' speech (1.2.68–73) because she can sense that this situation is about to escalate into even greater conflict and further public embarrassment? Or must she step in, because Hamlet's wordplay has humiliated and silenced his oafish uncle?

While it is tempting to characterize an intelligent Hamlet running circles around a dim-witted Claudius here, this is clearly not the case. It is not Hamlet who initiates the antagonism of their initial exchanges, but Claudius, and not simply by converting Hamlet from his 'cousin' to his 'son' with a regal wafting of a newly sceptred hand, but by employing a distinctly acerbic wordplay in then asking,

'How is that the clouds still hang on you?' (1.2.66). Aside from being insensitively blunt about Hamlet's persistent (though potentially embarrassing) state of mourning, this question works at being doubly offensive by transforming Hamlet's black clothes into ignoble and filthy 'clouts' (rags), to which Hamlet responds with his own pun about being too much in the sun (rather than in his clouds/clouts). We can see why Gertrude interrupts this exchange of blows. Yet it is Claudius who has the last word in this. Picking up on the final phrase of Hamlet's morally and rhetorically grand 'I know not seems' speech, Claudius begins his second long monologue of this scene with a show of diplomacy, by turning Hamlet's 'suits of woe' into a sign of Hamlet's 'sweet and commendable' nature (1.2.86–87). This move allows Claudius to reassert a rhetoric of equal measures that has been knocked temporarily off-balance by Hamlet's verbal spannering: the Prince's woeful 'suit' thus becomes 'sweet', in a nature now glossed by Claudius as 'commendable' (which is hardly how Hamlet has revealed himself so far). Far from being a proffered olive branch, though, the speech that follows (1.2.87–117) is a show of rhetorical force the savagery of which is sharpened by the calmness with which we might imagine Claudius delivering it, as he presents to Hamlet a sermon on grief not just to comfort but also to humiliate the Prince, with its language of a 'filial obligation' being countered by 'obsequious sorrow'; of an 'obstinate condolement' reflecting an 'impious stubbornness'; and telling of a 'heart unfortified' and a 'mind impatient'. Hamlet's show of mourning is attacked in almost unthinkable terms for a formal, courtly, public address: it is denounced (albeit very coolly) as 'unmanly', 'unschooled', 'peevish', and 'To reason most absurd'. Yet all of these insults are cast within a style designed to display, more than anything else, Claudius's own rationality, balance and even-handedness as Hamlet's new father and his king.

Most effective, though, is how this long, quietly but forcefully retaliatory homily burns towards its final line. Although Claudius makes a virtue of declaring publicly that Hamlet is now 'the most immediate to our throne' (1.2.109), nevertheless his real point is made clear only when Claudius proclaims Hamlet once more (and with a victorious rhetorical flourish) 'Our chiefest courtier, cousin, and our son' (l. 117). The purpose of this speech all along has been to finish what Claudius started to pronounce some 50 lines earlier, before being interrupted by Hamlet's shifty quips about 'kin' and 'kind', 'sons' and 'suns'. In this way, the King forces on Hamlet his new, and impossible, identity as 'our [. . .] cousin, and our son' whether the Prince likes it or not, trapping Hamlet within the rhetorical boxes Claudius has already prepared for him. No wonder Hamlet seethes with such anger and despair when left alone on stage for the first time just a few lines later. For under a veneer of hard consolation and soft chastisement, the King throws Hamlet very publicly in 1.2, pinning him beneath a heavyweight combination of clever rhetoric and cunning insults, and pronouncing the Prince as his 'son' whether Hamlet accepts it or not. How do we read Hamlet's silence at this point? Why does he not respond? Who has silenced whom?

The reverberations of these exchanges between Hamlet and the King can certainly be felt throughout the rest of the play. The fact that Hamlet is persuaded not to go 'back to school in Wittenberg' (1.2.113), but to stay in Denmark (where Claudius can keep a close eye upon him, presumably), does not ease the King's mistrust of him, or make it any easier for him to comprehend Hamlet's 'drift' from this point onwards. Equally, Hamlet's own actions throughout *Hamlet* suggest that the humiliation of 1.2, and the force with which Claudius entraps him there as 'my cousin, and my son', never leaves him. In Hamlet's few subsequent exchanges with Claudius (they rarely speak to one another again), Hamlet circles back to the terms of these painful opening exchanges, despite the fact that the King avoids referring to Hamlet as his 'son' again, at least until he is assured of Hamlet's death in 5.2 (l. 269), unlike the King of the 1603 First Quarto *Hamlet*, who antagonizes Hamlet as his 'son' throughout (*Hamlet* 2006b, 55, n.26). When they next address each other after 1.2, before the play is performed in 3.2, Claudius's more tentative enquiry, 'How fares our cousin Hamlet?' (3.2.88), is followed by a brief dialogue that effectively takes up where the banter of 1.2 left off, with Hamlet chopping Claudius's words into heavily loaded nonsense about 'air' (and thus 'heir'): all a very meaningful 'nothing' (see 3.2.88–95).

But it is in Hamlet's last words with Claudius in 4.3, just before leaving for England, that Hamlet flashes his last retort at being called Claudius's 'son' in 1.2, by comically bidding the King 'Farewell, dear mother' (4.3.48). While the joke here is that 'Father and mother is man and wife' and that 'Man and wife is one flesh. So – my mother' (4.3.49–50), the purpose of these words is not just to draw out, yet again, the problem of Claudius's marriage to Gertrude, and of the confusions of 'kin' and 'kind' that result from their status as 'one flesh', or even to expose the hypocrisy of Claudius as a pretended 'loving father' who is about to send his 'cousin' and his 'son' to his death (4.3.48). It is also to throw back at Claudius a twisted form of the rhetorical smugness the King displayed in 1.2. If Hamlet is to be addressed as both 'cousin' and 'son', then Claudius leaves himself open to be insulted as both his 'mother' and 'father', by virtue of the same 'incestuous' problem: his marriage to Gertrude. Hamlet appears to have been waiting a long time to finish this particular wrangle with his 'uncle-father' (2.2.313), and to make this bitter joke face-to-face, in order to gain something like the last word. In itself, this might suggest a structure at play in *Hamlet* which is darkly comedic. For as the jester, Feste, likewise demonstrates at the vengeful close of Shakespeare's comedy *Twelfth Night*, it is in just this way that 'the whirligig of time brings in his revenges' (5.1.366–7). Hamlet – another wise Shakespearean fool – knows this routine all too well.

UNHAPPY FAMILIES

The conflict and rivalry of Hamlet and Claudius puts into deeper perspective the complexity of the play's other secondary roles, most of whom stand somewhere between the polarized characters of the Prince and the King, as well as in complicated relationship to one another. The characters of Polonius and Laertes, Gertrude and Ophelia play crucial roles in reflecting the character of Claudius's court, and in signalling the play's discomfiting claustrophobia when it comes to the close ties of family and the enclosing affairs of state. Naturally, they also put into relief something of the character of the Prince. Polonius and Laertes, for example, may appear to occupy roles in *Hamlet* that work primarily as counterparts or doubles of the Prince. As Ophelia's father, convinced that Hamlet's 'transformation' has its roots in romantic rejection by his daughter, Polonius appears at key points to become the 'straight man' to (and ultimately the fall guy of) Hamlet's 'mad' scenes. When on stage with Polonius, then, Hamlet's 'antic disposition' establishes itself most clearly as akin to that of a professional 'fool' like Feste, mocking this 'tedious old fool' through a quick-fire comedy of satirical wordplay and absurdist sketch routines. It is in this manner that Polonius himself comes to be 'tendered' as the real 'fool' of the play (a 'rash, intruding fool' and 'a most foolish prating knave', even in death it seems (3.4.29, 213)), the two parts thus counterbalancing each other throughout around this keyword: fool.

Laertes is an even more obvious counterbalance to Hamlet. It is Laertes who seems to expose Hamlet's ineffectiveness as an avenger most effectively, for example, by taking on the character of hot-blooded revenger himself, and without any hesitation. He storms into the court in 4.5, threatening 'rebellion' and destruction with 'giant-like' ferocity (l. 121), vowing 'allegiance' to 'the blackest devil' and daring 'damnation' (ll. 130, 132), before declaring: 'Let come what comes, only I'll be revenged / Most throughly for my father' (ll. 134–5). Although Polonius's untimely demise is public knowledge in a way that old Hamlet's is not (making it easier for Laertes to make a 'riotous' scene of his revenge, and with the support of the 'rabble', in a way young Hamlet simply cannot (4.5.100–2)), nevertheless we may be thinking at this point that at last *Hamlet* has its revenge hero. Is not this exactly how Hamlet should have behaved all along? Yet the rivalry between these vengeful sons is established long before Laertes returns in 4.5. He is conspicuously privileged by Claudius in 1.2 (being given the King's attention long before he addresses the Prince, here), and is shown warning Ophelia to 'fear' the seductions of Hamlet in 1.3, and to think 'no more' upon him. With both Polonius and Ophelia dead by 5.1, Shakespeare capitalizes spectacularly upon the web of irony that has brought about enmity between these two, by having them fight over (or perhaps even in) Ophelia's grave in 5.1, and – more formally and fatally – in the match of 5.2. When Hamlet quips 'I'll be your foil, Laertes' (5.2.232), as they choose their 'foils' in the play's final scene, it is as if we have been waiting for someone to notice this since 1.2. Whether wrestling over Ophelia's corpse, or in exchanging bitter courtesies before their swordplay begins, it seems that we regard Hamlet and Laertes as mirror images: they appear not so much as enemies, but as brothers.

Because Hamlet, Polonius, and Laertes form a triangle linked by their interest in Ophelia, and by the play's focus on father–son relationships, we can see how Shakespeare intertwines the dramatic plotlines and structural motifs of these three characters to great effect. But to see Polonius and Laertes in these terms alone – merely as 'foils' for the Prince – can also be reductive. It would be easy to read Polonius and Laertes merely as 'types', with the former taking on the comical role of the easily duped father and busy old fool, and the latter taking on the part of the over-protective, jealous brother and angry young man (not to mention the damnation-daring revenger). To do so would be to absolve these parts of their own complexities and to side-step the way in which their roles inform the play's action in other ways. Both Polonius and Laertes occupy important positions, for instance, in the politic arrangements of the new king, a fact made emphatically clear by the obsequious way Claudius greets Laertes's 'suit' at 1.2.42–50, and which establishes Polonius's place as councillor-in-chief to 'the throne of Denmark'. As John Dover Wilson points out, Claudius 'positively coos' over Laertes at this point, 'caressing him with his first name four times in nine lines' (Wilson, 31), in a way that can only underscore our sense of Hamlet's marginalization further (who has yet to be spoken to at all by this point). This action also emphasizes how Polonius's character is first framed by his close political identification with Claudius. He is the new regime's right-hand man – the King's first minister – and as such his son receives special privileges, over and above those available even to the Prince who, unlike Laertes, is not granted permission to leave Elsinore, but is pressed to stay in 1.2.

While instinctively our first question about Polonius might be whether he has been an accomplice in the murder of old Hamlet (it would be natural, perhaps, to consider this as a possibility), Polonius's concerns over the Prince subsequently seem far from politic: Polonius worries over Hamlet's behaviour as the father of a daughter, not as a councillor concerned with any likely attempt on the throne. Yet he is still far from the benevolent old fool we might assume him to be. Polonius is powerful enough politically to sanction and organize the covert surveillance of Hamlet, and ruthless enough to press his own daughter into this service. He even takes the liberty of secreting himself in the Queen's private chamber (not her bedroom, but her 'closet') in 3.4, after giving Gertrude some 'round' instructions as to how to proceed with her own son in this scene (see 3.4.1–5). Polonius evidently (and surprisingly) has the power to direct the Queen as easily he does his own 'green girl' (1.3.100) of a daughter in such affairs. Equally, it is not just Polonius's treatment of Ophelia (whom he instructs not to have any more dealings with Hamlet in 1.3, but then uses her as chief prop in the entrapment scene of 3.1), that remains problematic but of Laertes too, when we discover in 2.1 that he is to be spied upon (and even scandalized) in Paris by Polonius's hired hand, Reynaldo.

Who and what Polonius is, then, is far from clear: old fool, sinister accomplice, politician, spy, an overbearing or an over-caring father? As Michael Pennington puts it, his character naturally brings into focus some 'bleak interpretative choices', as Polonius's part seems to be divided into clear 'polarities': he is both 'a Machiavellian public man, authoritarian with his family, but beneath it sexually prurient', and at the same time 'a capable professional and a loving father' (48–9; 48, n.22). Polonius 'in one aspect' is 'a comic busybody' whose 'wisdom', as R.A. Foakes suggests, is never 'simply despicable, since it is so much bound up with service and loyalty to the state', and yet 'in another he is the prototype of the director of a Central Intelligence Agency, eager to find dirt, to gather information he can use to bully Ophelia, confirm his worst suspicions about Laertes, or reveal the cause of Hamlet's madness' (Foakes 1993, 162). How we determine 'what Polonius is' could well be crucial to our reading of *Hamlet* because, as Pennington notes, his character 'reveals much about Claudius's court' and 'affects the balance of sympathies between Hamlet and himself – and therefore the quality of the play's comedy', as well as how we view 'Ophelia's decline into madness and the character of his son's rebellion' (Pennington, 48). It can hardly be said that Polonius's role is simply to provide a focus for Hamlet's antic knavery, or that Hamlet is the only complex or 'discontinuous' figure of the play. Polonius is, rather, among the play's longest and most densely layered parts.

Something of this ambivalence touches all of the central secondary figures in *Hamlet* in a way that makes even relatively minor roles take on a depth and magnitude the significance of which often outstrips the number of lines a character is given to speak. Laertes has a small role to play in *Hamlet*, then, but his part is made significant by virtue of being not just Hamlet's double but also Polonius's and Claudius's. It is in Laertes that the King finds a surrogate son and a new right-hand man to fill the place vacated by Polonius from 4.5 onwards, as well as someone who will act out his own villainy – to take Claudius's place, in that sense – in plotting the murder of Hamlet in Act 5. From 4.7, Laertes thus comes to represent, as much as his father may have done, all that is suspect and corrupt about Claudius's regime, and it is in Laertes that Hamlet finds an instrument with which to destroy that regime and complete his own revenge. The complexity of Laertes's character – as briefly delineated as it is in the play – is thus generated not just by his own traits (of vengeful villainy and treachery, for example, alongside those of honour and valour) but also by the way the play's 'implicit role repetitions' invite us 'to build perceptual bridges between and among characters', and to read them as 'parts of the same dynamic environment' (States, 103). Hence, in his three scenes with Ophelia (alive in 1.3, mad in 4.5, and dead in 5.1), Laertes's displays of intense concern, affection and passion make him appear more of a rival lover to Hamlet than a brother to Ophelia. His part thus adumbrates further the unsettling feeling we may have that incest in the world of *Hamlet* is never far beneath the surfaces of its characters' desires, whether between Claudius and his 'sometime sister', Gertrude, or between Laertes and Ophelia, into whose grave her brother leaps, refusing to see his sister's corpse interred 'Till I have caught her once more in mine arms' (5.1.239) (Lacan; States, 119).

It is through Laertes's character, then, as much as through *Hamlet*'s focus on the 'incestuous' marriage of Claudius and Gertrude, that we can start to see how easy it would be to make another Freudian leap into sensing that the incestuous heat of Oedipal desire may be smouldering between the Prince and his mother. Indeed, it is because of the heavyweight sexual speculation that surrounds *Hamlet*'s only two women, Gertrude and Ophelia, and especially in their relationships with Hamlet, that they too become characters whose significance in the play seems to outweigh the extent of their speaking roles. It would be easy to think of Gertrude as arguably the most important character after Hamlet himself, for instance, not because her actions in the play are particularly significant, but because (as Janet Adelman points out) she is one of Shakespeare's few, fully drawn dramatic mothers (mothers often remaining absent from Shakespearean dramatic families), and because she appears from the outset to be the focus of Hamlet's own despair and disgust (Adelman, 11–37). What is astonishing about Hamlet's first soliloquy (as we explored in Chapter 1) is how Gertrude rather than Claudius bears the brunt of his raw resentment. While Hamlet's exasperation and bewilderment in this soliloquy dismiss Claudius as a mere 'satyr' by comparison to the 'Hyperion' that was his father, it is Gertrude who is characterized more damnably here as sexually culpable, if not grotesque in 'appetite'. She is worse than a 'beast', it seems, given the 'wicked speed' and 'dexterity' with which, Hamlet tells us, she leaped so soon after her husband's death ('Within a month') between 'incestuous sheets' (1.2.129–59).

We get a taste of this disgust in Hamlet's first words to Gertrude in 1.2 – 'Ay, madam, it is common' (l. 74) – which, among its other densely packed puns, implicitly pins on her a whorish reputation for being 'common' (sexually available to all). It is to this alleged promiscuity and sexual voracity that Hamlet returns again in the 'closet scene' of 3.4, when he instructs her (at least twice) to 'go not to my uncle's bed' (3.4.157; 180–6), which is transformed here into a 'nasty sty', 'enseamed' and 'Stewed in corruption' (3.4.89–91). Such terms alone must give psychoanalysts of Hamlet's character plenty to think about. But where does this leave us in terms of reading Gertrude's character? On one level, it is easy to see how Gertrude's role in *Hamlet* gains a particular status primarily in relation to the Prince himself, becoming a blank page upon which some of Hamlet's inferred anxieties are projected. As Adelman puts it, Gertrude's 'presence' has a 'devastating impact' upon the Prince (Adelman, 11–15), inspiring diatribes against her in 1.2 and 3.4 which appear to reveal something about Hamlet's attitude towards sex and sexuality, and especially towards women, who are famously aligned in Hamlet's first soliloquy with 'frailty' (with sexual and moral weakness). One of the dramatic functions of *Hamlet*'s women seems to beg the question once again of what Hamlet's 'problem' might really be. Equally, though, Hamlet's characterization of Gertrude as sexually 'wicked', bestial and 'common' in itself points towards a series of uncertainties about the Queen left to be filled with other kinds of speculation. Is Gertrude not just sexually 'frail', but adulterous, for instance? Does her speedy marriage to the new king imply that the royal couple had been 'at it' before the old king was murdered (as is the case with the Gerutha of Belleforest's account of Amleth, for example, and which the Ghost seems to imply in his references to her 'falling off' (1.5.47) in his ghastly narrative of 1.5)? Is Gertrude an accomplice in the murder of Hamlet's father, as Hamlet ventures in the 'closet scene' (3.4.26–7)? If not, how could she be unaware of the murder? And is her alleged sexual appetite a sign that Gertrude is capable of producing an heir for Claudius, one who might well oust Hamlet's status as 'most immediate to our throne'?[1]

The importance of such questions lies not in how they might finally be answered, but in the fact that the play pushes us into considering them in the first place. As a result, Gertrude becomes something of an unknown quantity as a 'character', taking centre stage in the drama of Hamlet's doubts and suspicions, without necessarily answering or allaying them. Unlike the Queen of the 1603 First Quarto *Hamlet*, who in an equivalent 'closet scene' (*Hamlet* 2006b, scene 11) declares outright that she has no knowledge of old Hamlet's murder (11.85–6), and vows unequivocally to 'assist' her son in his revenge (11.95–100), Gertrude's attitude to Hamlet and Claudius in the Second Quarto and Folio texts (and thus of most modern editions) is much more difficult to fathom. Following the 'closet scene', does Gertrude now believe that Claudius is a murderer, or does she consider her son to be a proper madman, prone to rash stabbings and hallucinations? Can Hamlet's performance in 3.4 really persuade her to forsake her husband's bed, or her loyalty to the King? Whose side is she on, we might wonder. Gertrude's unreadability as a character leaves her open to particular kinds of inference, with which film-makers and psychoanalytic critics have done much. In becoming Hamlet's creature of uncontrollable sexuality, Gertrude can step forward as the determining and blameable figure in Hamlet's Oedipal drama of conflict, guilt and delay, as well as a mother whose guilt and sexuality could be shown to spill luridly into her own relationship with her son in performance, through seductive looks, open-mouthed kisses, and the all-important interpolation of a bed in the Queen's 'closet' of 3.4.[2]

The problem with approaching Gertrude's character in this way is obvious. If we regard Gertrude solely from Hamlet's perspective, she all too quickly becomes frozen into the stereotypical roles of lusting widow, or conniving, untrustworthy villainess, or the seductress of some Oedipal nightmare. As with other secondary figures, it seems that we have to resist reading Gertrude's character through Hamlet's descriptions alone, and weigh them against the part otherwise presented in the play. Because Hamlet offers us a version of his mother's character based upon actions taken in the past – namely her hasty marriage to Claudius, the motivation for which is much less clear than Hamlet supposes – then reading the character of Gertrude according to what she does and says in the dramatic present of the play allows us to see someone quite different. Gertrude seems to display no sexual voracity whatsoever, and any opportunity to do so is limited in any case by the few times that she and Claudius actually appear together in the play, being alone on stage as a couple just once (for less than 30 lines in 4.1). Gertrude's part seems to be characterized most often by an ability to mediate in awkward moments of conflict, intervening in the wrangling of husband and son in 1.2, and crucially once again when Laertes storms the court in 4.5, threatening the King's person. It is to an albeit reluctant Gertrude, then, that Elsinore turns first to comfort the mad Ophelia, and to 'speak with her' in her distraction (4.5.1).

Yet, while she is present at key moments in the play's action, Gertrude's story is also one of gradual neutralization as a figure of political importance. Whereas she and Claudius act and speak together in the early scenes of the play (1.2, 2.2), sharing one politic voice, by 3.1 she is quite clearly sidelined by Claudius and Polonius, who dismiss her in order to spy upon Hamlet and Ophelia alone. Her response here – 'I shall obey you' (3.1.36) – is wide open to interpretation: is this submissive or reluctant, frustrated or sarcastic, disillusioned or disempowered? Her role in such affairs is diminished further from this point, as she becomes little more than a decoy herself in the closet scene of 3.4. Coupled with what appear to be characteristic modes of speech (addressing others around her as 'Good', for example: 'Good Hamlet', 'Good gentlemen' (1.2.68; 2.2.19)), Gertrude's place in the sequence of the play's action (as an astute and perceptive queen, a sensitive reader of others' moods) seems quite distinct from Hamlet's characterization of her as a 'wicked' monster, or a sexually depraved 'beast'. It is between these two poles – how Hamlet sees her and the part the play gives her – that we are asked to think again about who and what the character of Hamlet's mother might be. As Rebecca Smith notes, 'Gertrude's words and actions in Shakespeare's *Hamlet* create not the lusty, lustful, lascivious Gertrude that one generally sees in stage and film productions', nor even the 'strong woman' of the play reclaimed by other critics, 'but a compliant, loving, unimaginative woman whose only concern is pleasing others' (Smith, 91, and see Ouditt).

Such a Gertrude may not seem, of course, much of an improvement upon A.C. Bradley's half-hearted description of her, delivered over a century ago, as 'not a bad-hearted woman' (Bradley, 141), or upon T.S. Eliot's damning account of her as 'so negative and insignificant' that she seems 'incapable' of arousing Hamlet's passions, or our own (Eliot, 101). As Bert O. States puts it, even 'Osric is more interesting to watch' than Gertrude, while acknowledging that 'it takes considerable finesse to create a character who arouses questions for which coherent answers are not forthcoming' (rather like Hamlet, one might think), yet who must also remain understated and indeed uninteresting, 'lest we begin to think about the critical question surrounding her character: how much does she know?' (States, 106). Yet Gertrude's inactivity and blankness may make no difference whatsoever to the crime of which she is 'guilty' from Hamlet's perspective: of being a woman whose remarriage has 'effectively cut off Hamlet from his hereditary entitlement' (Jardine 1983, 92) to the throne of Denmark. As Lisa Jardine puts it: 'Whether she has knowingly or unwittingly been drawn into Claudius's plot' does not matter, for whatever she does or does not do, Gertrude will always be suspect, 'by virtue of her power to disrupt the patriarchal power structure' in *Hamlet*, and the notion of 'patrilinear inheritance' in particular, *in spite of* her passivity' (Jardine 1983, 92–3; see also Adelman, 11–37, and de Grazia 2007, 81–128).

As the play's only other female character, Ophelia presents complexities both similar to and different from those of Gertrude. In many ways, she is clearly the Queen's counterpart in *Hamlet* (her 'reflection', as Jardine puts it), playing the young and sexually inexperienced (or even repressed) daughter to the latter's older, more worldly wise widow-wife-mother (Jardine 1983, 69). Both women form two sides of the emotionally charged dramatic triangle of Gertrude-Hamlet-Ophelia, then, and as such it is tempting to read Ophelia's role as significant only to the extent in which it too reveals something about Hamlet's character. Like his mother, Ophelia also becomes the target of Hamlet's indigestible sentiments at times, as well as the subject of his own contradictory confessions (he loves her in 5.1, but he loves her not in 3.1). Ophelia may thus appear to be a vehicle for the expression of Hamlet's (rather than her own) attitudes towards sexuality. Yet the two women are also linked – in mother-and-daughter fashion – by shared aspirations when it comes to Hamlet's relationship with Ophelia, in a way otherwise closed down by the play's tragic plot. It is Gertrude who in 3.1 and in 5.1 (amidst the play's cynical scheming and grief) articulates the hope and the sorrow that Ophelia and Hamlet might have been married, a possibility otherwise refused by the play's men and their more Machiavellian machinations (3.1.37–41; 5.1.232–5). Gertrude and Ophelia thus offer us glimpses of an alternative plot for Hamlet at the core of which stands a set of values contrary to those represented by Claudius, Polonius and Laertes, and also by Hamlet. *Hamlet's* two women together –

albeit subtly, but most definitely – form a centre of womanly solidarity and resistance within the play's otherwise male-dominated spheres of action.

Ophelia is also one of our principal sources of concern about and sympathy for Hamlet. While Gertrude is solicitous about Hamlet's well-being throughout the play, directing her enquiries about 'My too much changed son' (2.2.36) to Rosencrantz and Guildenstern in personal rather than political terms in 2.2 and 3.1, it is Ophelia who gives us the play's most detailed and rhetorically engaging expression of grief over Hamlet's tragic deterioration (and in soliloquy no less), having witnessed first-hand how 'Th'expectation and rose of the fair state, / The glass of fashion and the mould of form' is now 'quite, quite down' and 'Blasted with ecstasy' (3.1.151–3, 159). Given that Hamlet has just treated Ophelia in a way that has remained unconscionable to generations of readers and audiences of *Hamlet* (the 'get thee to a nunnery' speeches coming second in offensiveness only to his damnable soliloquy over the praying Claudius in 3.3, it seems), it is nevertheless Ophelia who, with great rhetorical poise and strength of mind, one might think, re-secures our sympathy all the more firmly for Hamlet at this point (see also Desmet 1992, 10–17). Claudius's immediate response to the very same scene – 'Love! His affections do not that way tend. / Nor what he spake [. . .] / Was not like madness' (3.1.161–3) – may be more astute, but it also reveals an insensitivity, a fatuousness, and a cynicism quite absent from Ophelia's distress. Without Ophelia (and likewise without Gertrude) we may simply not care about the Prince, or be able to perceive him as a character worth caring about. The role of these women in *Hamlet* is thus crucial: they create the dramatic space in which Hamlet's character can become worthy of our emotional as well as our dramatic engagement as a difficult 'hero'. One might think of them as the primary source of *Hamlet's* emotional intelligence as a drama.

Ophelia, however, is always in danger of appearing relatively *characterless*. This is in part because she appears to be subject to the commands and demands of others (namely her brother, father and her lover), rather than standing as a more fully defined or self-determining 'subject'. She is notably denied, then, the independence typical of a Shakespearean daughter-lover. In comparison to her rebellious sisters of other early modern dramas (such as Hermia in *A Midsummer Night's Dream* or Jessica in *The Merchant of Venice*, or even Juliet and Desdemona, albeit to tragic effect in their plays), Ophelia simply does not act according to type. Rather than defying the injunctions of Laertes and Polonius in the name of love's higher authority, Ophelia obeys them. As a result, she is left appearing merely passive, uninteresting and vacant. 'I do not know, my lord, what I should think' (1.3.103) could be the sum of Ophelia's 'character', one might think, with her on-stage role rallying into active agency only in the more spectacular 'flower' scenes of her madness and grief in 4.5. As Pennington puts it, 'as the character [of Ophelia] looks down her abyss, the part looks up'. 'Poor Ophelia' indeed, we might conclude (Pennington, 165, 48).

Yet, as ever, we should be wary of surmising too much too soon concerning a character about whom we see, hear and know so little. Ophelia is denied the option of becoming the rebellious female of her father's household less through any weakness of 'character', perhaps, than by the fundamental unreliability of Hamlet as her lover. Unlike Romeo, Othello, or Lysander in their plays, Hamlet is unavailable to her as a stable romantic hero or as a potential husband: his show of madness (feigned or not) cancels the possibility for Ophelia of an alternative romance plot. What also makes Ophelia's character appear problematically, and atypically, passive is how she is given so little space in the play, both in terms of her appearances on stage (a mere five in total), and in relation to her claustrophobic familial situation. While Laertes and Polonius intrude upon her thoughts and feelings openly – demanding to know and then to cancel or control them in 1.3 – Hamlet likewise intrudes upon her in the private space of her 'closet' (as Ophelia describes it at 2.1.74), in a way replicated in 3.1. Trapped between the intrusive surveillance of Claudius and Polonius and the extreme bipolarity of Hamlet's evasive 'antic disposition' (instructing her to 'get thee to a nunnery' in one scene, and making crudely sexual jokes about 'country matters' in the next), Ophelia is given little room either to respond in these situations or to act other than as a staged property in the drama of observation and mistrust being acted out by the men around her. Her dead body brought on stage in 5.1 might seem little more than an extension of her role as a theatricalized object throughout *Hamlet*, being positioned marionette-like by her director-father in 3.1, and made partner to Hamlet's display of sexual giddiness in 3.2. The small space of the grave that awaits her in 5.1 seems emblematic not just of Hamlet's preoccupations with women, sex and death (as we might suppose), but also of how the action of Hamlet's tragedy has enclosed Ophelia in restrictive, deadening and finally deadly ways from the very beginning.

As the focus of and a medium for the play's challenging treatment of women, Ophelia's final display of sexualized mindlessness in 4.5 may seem representative of a character who throughout the play has been emptied of significance in everything other than sexual terms by those around her. While Ophelia's bawdy songs and puns in the flower-giving scenes of 4.5 might reflect 'the necessarily discordant nature of her sexuality' (Lyons 1977, 62), signalling a sense of liberty and release otherwise unavailable to her in the play while sane, this madness cannot be mistaken as a form of empowerment. In her madness, Ophelia is not afforded the opportunity of becoming a more interesting or fully developed character, in the way that Hamlet's feigned show of 'antics' works for him. Rather, it threatens to empty her of 'character', by transforming her into a dramatic spectacle, making her a spectral Ophelia, and a non-character: 'a vacuum where there once was a person', an 'empty space', a 'nothing' (Showalter, 91). Such is Ophelia's tragedy: to become more of a problem of 'iconography' in her madness and death rather than an imitation of humanity in its fullest sense. Subsequently, she is more easily dealt with by those in the play (as well as by her detractors, defenders and admirers outside it), as something other than a dramatic person or a 'character', becoming more conveniently an icon: whether of pastoral innocence and child-like experience stained by grief, as Gertrude depicts her (4.7.164–81), or of the patriarchal oppression of all of Shakespeare's daughters (Lyons; Jardine 1983, 72–3; Showalter; Ronk).

ENEMIES AND FRIENDS

Like Ophelia, other characters in *Hamlet* can also be seen taking on emblematic or symbolic qualities, their importance in the play residing either in their visual impact or in the way that their presence, however fleeting or temporary, has lasting and powerful effects, amplifying the play's action and its structures of meaning in profound ways. In Act 5, for instance, the introduction of two Clowns (as the gravediggers are identified in the first printed versions of *Hamlet*) provide a dark comedy designed not to relieve the tragedy of its grimness, but to intensify and complicate it. Their quips and songs bookend Hamlet's own deadly clowning as an 'antic' figure, while their jocularity in digging Ophelia's grave reminds us just how deliberately Shakespeare is testing the boundaries of generic convention and decorum in *Hamlet*, mixing clowns and kings, jesters and princes, laughter and death to startling dramatic effect. Much could be said of almost all the minor characters of *Hamlet*, though. Such is the dramatic economy of Shakespeare's longest play that every part can be considered resonant with significance, from the nervous soldiers on watch in 1.1 to the company of players appearing in 2.2, to the unexpected emergence in 5.2 of that verbally corrupt 'water-fly', Osric: a courtier well-studied in the new regime's morally bankrupt verbosity.

Two figures who demand special attention, despite the brevity of their walk-on parts, are young Fortinbras and the Ghost. They are counterparts to one another in many ways, appearing (by and large) at the beginning and at the end of *Hamlet*, and thus framing the action as visual reminders of a heroic, masculine, martial ethos against which Hamlet's own character as a prince, along with the nature of Claudius's regime, can be measured (Foakes 1993, 146–80; and Foakes 2005). This point of contrast and continuity would be particularly effective if Fortinbras (visiting Elsinore on his way back to Norway, having 'with conquest come from Poland' (5.2.334)) were to enter 5.2 dressed in armour, ready for war and armed in a way that the Ghost appears to be dressed in Act 1. Both the Ghost and Fortinbras are war-like doubles of each other. But they are also doubles of Hamlet, and for this reason they build some key 'perceptual bridges' across the play's 'dynamic environment', as States suggests (103), while establishing some conceptual foundations for it.

It is easy to imagine, for instance, a production of *Hamlet* which removes Fortinbras's role entirely. This is, in fact, what Olivier's 1948 film does. As a *Hamlet* without the Prince (of Norway, that is), Olivier's cinematic adaptation is able to focus on the play as a drama primarily of mind and psychology, with any events happening beyond the labyrinthine corridors and dark spaces of Elsinore (depicted as a reflection of Hamlet's own torturous thinking in the film) being erased from the play's world, and never intruding upon it. Erasing Fortinbras, then, can intensify the claustrophobia of *Hamlet*'s atmosphere significantly. Yet without Fortinbras we are bereft of a key political context for the play's events (which are taking place against the backdrop of international conflict and uncertainties over land and succession), as well as of a central contrasting figure for Hamlet who serves also as a powerful focus of the plot's tragic irony. Stepping onto the stage in 5.2 to take Denmark's crown in a tragic instant, Fortinbras suddenly exceeds his role as a son originally intent upon regaining those lands lost by his dead father (as he is presented to us in the opening speech of 1.2). In so doing, he marks a full turn of the wheel. For it is not young Hamlet who inherits the throne of Denmark, but his döppelganger, young Fortinbras, whose father (old Fortinbras) was killed by Hamlet's father (old Hamlet) on the very day young Hamlet was born (as the gravedigger informs us in 5.1.135–40). The whirligig of time certainly does bring in its revenges. Without young Fortinbras, this dimension of the tragedy simply would not register. Unsurprisingly, Fortinbras's declaration that Hamlet would 'have proved most royal' had he lived, and so deserves to be given full military honours by being borne 'like a soldier to the stage' (5.2.380, 382), present some final problems when it comes to reading both his and Hamlet's characters. Fortinbras's last words are too easily undercut by irony: they give us an honourable (is it or the opportunist's?) view of a martial Hamlet whom we simply may not recognize, coming from the mouth of a character whom we have never really met before (only briefly in 4.4), and who, as far as we can tell, does not even know the dead prince before him.

The Ghost presents a different order of puzzling. Like the part of Fortinbras, we may be uncertain whether the Ghost qualifies as a 'character' at all. While John Dover Wilson regarded it as 'a character [. . .] in the fullest sense of the term', in that it 'retains a human heart' and 'a touch of pathos' despite its distant 'stateliness' and 'majesty' (Wilson, 52), more recent commentators have seen the Ghost as exemplary of all that makes 'character' such a complex dramatic concept. As Jonathan Holmes has summarized, because an actor playing the Ghost 'is not bound by any ideas of consistency of characterisation, because [. . .] in a sense, there is no character' to play, then the Ghost itself 'becomes the epitome of all stage characterisations, a presence comprised of absence, a physicality without psychology': it represents, then, 'a literalisation of the process of constructing character' which is explored throughout the play (Holmes, 102, 105). *Hamlet*'s interest in identity and selfhood, in what constitutes 'character', thus has its roots in the play's most ambiguous and spectacular figure who, in being everywhere and nowhere, some 'thing' and yet nothing, anticipates the complexity of young Hamlet himself as a dramatic person, for whom the Ghost stands as yet another (perhaps a metadramatic) spectral self. G. Wilson Knight gets it quite startlingly wrong, then, in assuming that it is the Prince who 'is the only discordant element, the only hindrance to happiness, health, and prosperity' in 'the universe of this play', standing on the stage as 'a living death in the midst of life' (Knight, 40). There is perhaps no better way of describing the Ghost that appears in 1.1 than this.

Such is the Ghost's significance in the play that it too could be considered the most important secondary part. It is the Ghost, after all, who (though appearing far more like a 'real' ghost than the kind of spectral Chorus one might otherwise expect to find in a revenge tragedy) bequeaths to Hamlet his revenge. Yet the problems presented by Hamlet's task are in part also due to this Ghost of 'questionable shape' (1.4.43). On the one hand, the Ghost gives Hamlet mixed signals – if not contradictory or double-bind instructions – in its commands of 1.5: Hamlet must both revenge his father's murder, and yet make the command 'remember me' his priority; he must take revenge yet not 'Taint' his 'mind' in the process; he must kill his uncle, yet 'contrive' nothing against his mother, despite the fact that Gertrude is as guilty as Claudius, according to the Ghost's account (see 1.5.84–91). On the other hand, as we addressed in Chapter 2, the Ghost is Hamlet's only witness and his sole body of evidence in the case of his father's murder. In being given information upon which he cannot immediately act, it is hardly surprising that Hamlet is left 'unpregnant' of his 'cause' by the end of 2.2 (l. 503). But the real problem of the Ghost also emerges from this puzzle, as we have seen. Can it be trusted? More to the point: what is this 'thing'? The spirit of Hamlet's father, or a devil in his father's likeness (as Hamlet speculates in the soliloquy of 2.2)? Is it a benevolent or a malevolent Ghost? A 'spirit of health or goblin damned' (1.4.40)? Does it grant to Hamlet a divinely sanctioned role as an instrument of God's justice, or does it make the Prince a victim of the infernal?

The Ghost's significance lies not simply in complicating the action of revenge in *Hamlet* nor, in a way that may now seem equally obvious, in forming a key element in Hamlet's Oedipal drama (if that is what we think this play gives us). Rather, its impact lies in the uncertainty it generates as an unidentifiable 'thing' (which is how the characters in 1.1 initially describe it), and in breathing a sense of deep unease throughout *Hamlet* about what is knowable or not, and what is 'real' or not. The ontological illegibility of the Ghost registered by its witnesses in Act 1, including the 'scholar' Horatio, thus informs our own speculative responses both to it and to the rest of the action. Is this a devil that simply looks like old Hamlet, as we are reminded repeatedly, or is it the actual 'spirit' of Hamlet's warlike father? Are its intentions honourable, or demonic? Is it a Catholic spirit, as its references to purgatorially 'sulphurous and tormenting flames' (1.5.3) might suggest? If so, this spirit of the 'Old Faith' requests a Protestant Hamlet (a student of Wittenberg, we should remember: see Chapter 1) to perform the deeply un-Christian task of revenge. How yet another murder would alleviate the pains of purgatory (the existence of which was refuted by Protestants as a 'fable') is never quite clear.[3] Or is the problem, here, that the Ghost straddles an uncertain dramatic identity, being both a Christianized spirit suffering for its own 'foul crimes' and, at the same time, a conventional figure of Classical revenge tragedy, and thus essentially pagan in its desire to see revenge accomplished? Everything about the Ghost, from its strained, antique rhetoric of being murdered when 'Unhouseled, disappointed, unaneled' (1.5.77) to its seductive ability to speak to Hamlet's own obsession over 'incestuous' and 'adulterous' beasts polluting 'the royal bed of Denmark' (see 1.5.42–91), seems designed to reinforce our insecurity about its nature. The Ghost thereby establishes 'a pervasive pattern' in *Hamlet*, as Stephen Greenblatt puts it, marked by 'a deliberate forcing together of radically incompatible accounts of almost everything that matters in *Hamlet*', and which sends 'shock waves through the play' (Greenblatt 2001, 240).

As the Ghost does not return at the end of the play to offer any final commentary on the events we have seen (refusing to work as a Chorus in that sense), we can never be sure what it or its purposes finally are. Is it an ally or a fiend? A friend, finally, or an enemy? To frame the problem of the Ghost's 'identity' in such terms – either as friend or foe – may seem simplistic. Yet *Hamlet* appears to be structured around this dilemma from the outset: how to distinguish one's friends from one's enemies. Most notably, young Fortinbras – the chief enemy to Denmark at the beginning of the play, whose sabre-rattling has geared Elsinore into preparing for war (as we learn in 1.1) – appears in the final scene not just as a friend to Denmark, but most likely to become the next king, having won Hamlet's 'dying voice' in 'th'election' that must follow the play's disastrous denouement (5.2.339–40). Is Fortinbras's appearance in 5.2 simply fortuitous, then? Does it mark the diplomatic dropping-in of a former foe turned friendly neighbour? Or should we see his presence at Elsinore as indicative of an invasive threat from Denmark's time-honoured enemy, who stumbles upon a scene of tragedy in which his bloody work has already been done for him?

This kind of uncertainty is registered throughout the play, as *Hamlet*'s dialogue returns to the language of 'friends' and 'foes' at key points: we can find it in Claudius's wooing of Laertes as a 'friend' at 4.7.2, for example, or in the Player King's speech on how 'Fortune' makes 'friends of enemies' and vice versa (3.2.180–209), or in the way Rosencrantz and Guildenstern (Hamlet's oldest friends, 'being of so young days first brought up with him' (2.2.11)), are co-opted into spying on Hamlet by his enemy, Claudius, thus revealing themselves to be quite different from the Prince's 'excellent good friends' (as Hamlet initially greets them at 2.2.219). Even the play's opening question – 'Who's there?' – describes and inscribes this insecurity in the play (Evans, 88–90). The sentinels Barnardo and Francisco find it difficult at first to recognize each other or to be certain who should be challenging whom in 1.1, while watching for an enemy they know nothing about, in a war that has not yet been announced, and all the while nervous of some 'thing' appearing to them, the nature and meaning of which is as incomprehensible as everything else.

It is under these same circumstances that *Hamlet*'s other most important secondary figure, Horatio, first appears: a character traditionally perceived to be relatively uncomplicated (and, by the same token, not very interesting or even 'faceless' (States, 147)), but who serves primarily as Hamlet's most loyal and unambiguously 'good friend' (1.2.163). The play gives us good reason for thinking of 'Good Horatio' in these terms. He is Hamlet's 'only confidant' (de Grazia 2007, 90, 181), and his partner in detection and observation throughout the play. A fellow scholar of Wittenberg (and so having an affinity with Hamlet beyond the murky, familial entanglements of Claudius's court), Horatio is reliable and trustworthy, it seems. As one of the few characters to see the Ghost, he is aware from 1.5 that Hamlet's 'antic disposition' is feigned, and by 3.2 he has already been informed by Hamlet of 'the circumstance / [. . .] of my father's death' (3.2.72–3). By 5.2, Horatio is the only character really to know anything about Hamlet's actions and motivations, as well as of the King's foiled plot to have the Prince murdered in England. Horatio's special status is reinforced by Hamlet's crucial speech of 3.2, in which he declares how his friend has long been 'sealed' by his soul 'for herself' (ll. 59–61), as one who 'in suffering all' appears stoically as one 'that suffers nothing' (l. 62). Horatio, then, receives the prize of Hamlet's highest praise in the moving words (worthy of Shakespeare's Henry V, in fact): 'Give me that man / That is not passion's slave and I will wear him / In my heart's core – ay, in my heart of heart – / As I do thee' (3.2.67–70). Given that Hamlet speaks neither of nor to anyone else in the play with such sincerity and endearment, we can see why Hamlet breaks off at this point. There seems to be 'Something too much' (l. 70) in all of this for words to say. Such tender sentiment is articulated yet once more in the play only when the dying Prince bids Horatio: 'If thou didst ever hold me in thy heart / Absent thee from felicity awhile / And in this harsh world draw thy breath in pain / To tell my story' (5.2.330–3). Hamlet's lament over the dead Ophelia in 5.1 – in which he proclaims how 'forty thousand brothers / Could not with all their quantity of love / Make up my sum' (5.1.258–60) – seems prosaic and perfunctory (the language of an accountant, all numbers and sums) by comparison, confirming Hamlet's declaration in 3.2 that Horatio is nothing less than his soul's 'choice' and 'election' (3.2.59–60) (see Evans; MacFaul, 135–40).

Because Horatio affords Hamlet some rare opportunities to become 'himself' again (for as de Grazia observes, when addressing 'anyone other than his confidant Horatio' Hamlet is 'typically rude, offensive, or unintelligible', 181), then it is understandable how commentators have long characterized Horatio in idealized terms. While A.C. Bradley passes 'reluctantly' over this 'beautiful character' in order to address more important figures (Bradley, 140), Dover Wilson honours Horatio as Hamlet's 'bosom friend, a man he can entirely trust', and as 'the only friend he has in the world' (Wilson, 48–9, 79). He is, then, the Prince's 'one true friend' (Levin, 51). Though not a 'deep character', as Bert O. States remarks, nevertheless Horatio always seems 'nearby', and thus 'the one accountable certainty in a world of shifting confusions', offering Hamlet friendship without the suspicion that characterizes all of his other relationships in the play, and a 'genuine discourse' that 'avoids all trivial questions, including the central question of what has actually taken place' (States, 148–9).

In heroizing Horatio in these terms, though, we may be in danger of forgetting some of the other, more basic dramatic functions his character performs. Along with Gertrude and Ophelia, Horatio offers a key means of focusing on Hamlet as a figure who deserves our sympathy and pity. It is Horatio who breaks the news to Hamlet that his father's ghost has been witnessed stalking Elsinore's battlements, and it is he who voices concern over the Prince's well-being when invited to follow the Ghost in 1.4, and when again invited to match Laertes in the swordfight of 5.2. With the exception of the Prince's death, there is no moment more touching or more sad in all of *Hamlet* than that in which Horatio articulates his sense of Hamlet's doom in 5.2, saying simply and honestly, 'You will lose, my lord' (l. 187), before offering (as any good friend would) to 'forestall' the match with Laertes and 'say you are not fit', should Hamlet's 'mind dislike anything' (ll. 195–6), Hamlet having already confessed to him, of course, 'how ill all's here about my heart' (ll. 190–1). Horatio steps forward as Hamlet's 'good friend' at such points, becoming a sounding board of stoicism and reasonableness against which Hamlet's fatalism can be expressed and tested, when the Prince declares how his 'fate cries out' in following the Ghost (1.4.81), or when insisting that 'There is special providence in the fall of a sparrow' (5.2.197–202).

It is Horatio's rationality, scepticism and good will that allows our faith to be anchored in Hamlet as the play's 'hero', then, despite the Prince's alienating instability, passion, and madness (feigned or not). Horatio is thus the trustworthy companion to Hamlet in a way that sets a precedent for other dramatic double acts and literary partnerships to follow. Horatio is the play's figure of right reason, good judgement, and fair speaking more generally, though, as his name punningly implies: (Ho)-*ratio*, (H)-*oratio*, as well as Horatian (after the Roman poet, Horace). We find him advising everyone from the frightened soldiers of 1.1 to Gertrude in 4.5, to the fatalistic Hamlet of 5.2, and displaying always great urbanity and control. As the only character to have appeared (and survived) throughout the play from its first scene onwards, it seems right that the rational Horatio should be left to bid his 'sweet Prince' goodnight at the end, and to 'speak to th'yet unknowing world / How these things came about' (5.2.363–4), just as he was bidden to 'speak' to the mysterious Ghost in 1.1. Who else could do so, other than him?

Yet all is not well when it comes to Horatio. The question of 'enemy or friend?' is more difficult to answer in his case than we might think. He is certainly far from being 'the one accountable certainty in a world of shifting confusions' (States, 148), being as susceptible as any other character to inconsistency and 'shiftiness'. What might be considered some of the play's most glaring dramatic inconsistencies surround Horatio, in fact, who is greeted by Hamlet in 1.2 as a stranger to Elsinore and to the customs of Denmark (having come from Wittenberg), and whom Hamlet seems barely to recognize at first, yet who also seems to know all about both Danish history and the possibility of a war with Norway in 1.1 (of which even the soldiers are ignorant), and who must logically have been in Denmark for quite some time, having come to attend old Hamlet's funeral (some two months before?). In which case, how have Hamlet and Horatio not met before 1.2? And how is that this outsider, a scholar of Wittenberg and a 'poor servant' to Hamlet (1.2.162), has become so deeply embedded in the world of the court by Act 4, that he can be found advising the Queen herself to speak to the mad Ophelia in 4.5, before being addressed as 'good Horatio' by Claudius in 5.1. He is even asked by the King to 'wait upon' Hamlet at this point, in a way reminiscent of the now dead Rosencrantz and Guildenstern (5.1.282). We may well wish to ask of Horatio, as of the Ghost or Gertrude, whose side is he actually on?

To raise these issues may appear to be retreading the tired ground of a kind of 'character criticism' most notably associated with A.C. Bradley. Questions such as 'Where was Hamlet at the time of his father's death?' (through which Bradley points out some of the problems with Horatio) are just the sort that he addresses in the appendices or 'Notes' of *Shakesperean Tragedy*, and which L.C. Knights (and F.R. Leavis, it seems) clearly had in mind when trashing his approach to 'character' in the essay 'How Many Children Had Lady Macbeth?' (Knights 1965) Yet it should be pointed out that such anomalies and inconsistencies do not concern questions of 'character' (nor are they addressed as such by Bradley) as much as the play's dramatic structuring. They could be dismissed either as unnoticeable in performance or, by contrast, as flaws in the surface of the play, which can be patched up in production as indications of 'bad construction', as Michael Pennington puts it (180). After all, part of Horatio's unusual prominence at court in 4.5 is textual, for in the Folio *Hamlet* he subsumes in his part (for reasons of economy, presumably) the lines of another part, which in the Second Quarto version belong to an anonymous 'Gentleman'. It is this 'Gentleman' in the 1604/05 text who asks the Queen to intervene in Ophelia's madness, rather than Horatio alone (as in the Folio text), whereas in the First Quarto of *Hamlet*, Horatio appears in another quite separate scene with the Queen (not replicated in the other versions) in which he informs her of Hamlet's escape from death in England, and thus signals his undivided loyalty to the Prince (*Hamlet* 2006b, 1603 text, scene 14). Like so much else in *Hamlet*, then, Horatio's 'inconsistency' may be a reflection of the text's, rather than his own, instability as a 'character'.

But Horatio's character should be let off neither on technicalities alone nor on the grounds that the 'difficulties' he presents 'really are a mark of failure' on Shakespeare's part, the dramatist having concentrated all his energies onto the Prince, as Pennington supposes (180). On the one hand, the kind of 'biographical logic' that Horatio seems to lack but which, according to Pennington, is 'much appreciated by actors and audiences' (180) is precisely the 'logic' against which all characterization works in *Hamlet*. Horatio's inconsistencies are no different from Hamlet's or even the Ghost's: they exemplify a process of character construction which defies 'unitary' or 'biographical' consistency. On the other hand, there is much more to the changing nature of Horatio's character than just Pennington's 'mark of failure' (180) in any case. Horatio's reactions to and treatment of Hamlet from 3.2 onwards (when we next see Horatio, after 1.5) mark a clear point of dramatic engagement: a shift in tone, role and sentiment for us to fathom. Whereas Horatio is the most voluble or talkative character of 1.1, and one of the key figures in Act 1 overall, when we see him in the graveyard of 5.1, it is almost as though we are dealing with an entirely different man: a servant of the Prince rather than a friend, and one whose former sociability and gregariousness has been replaced by tight-lipped servitude, as if he is merely humouring Hamlet's humours among the graves, having little more to say now than 'It might, my lord' and 'Ay, my lord' (5.1.76, 82).

A.D. Nuttall's 'penumbra of inferences' (2007, 176) darkens Horatio's character at this point, beyond any of the initial oddities and factual queries that surround his exchanges with Hamlet in 1.2. Why does Horatio not inform Hamlet of Ophelia's death in 5.1, for example? Is this an act of friendship? How do we read this particular silence, or Horatio's taciturn disposition more generally at the end of the play? Moreover, how do we read the tone of his responses to Hamlet's tale of adventure and escape during the 'sea-fight', recounted in 5.2, and the ambiguous statements Horatio utters here: 'So Guildenstern and Rosencrantz go to't' and 'Why, what a king is this!' (5.2.56, 61)? What is Horatio thinking when he offers Hamlet these words? Do they signal an 'implied closeness', through a willingness to 'criticise' and 'disagree' with Hamlet, 'a willingness which often signals true friendship', as one commentator suggests? (Evans, 116–17). Or do they signal something more unsettling? Can we be certain that Horatio is Hamlet's unambiguous friend? How are such lines to be spoken? And how, then, does Horatio say those famous – perhaps even impossible – words: 'Goodnight, sweet Prince' (5.2.343)? As much as the Ghost, as much as the Prince, Horatio is not just a 'character' in *Hamlet*: he too is a question mark in the shape of a man.

THROUGH THE CHARACTERS TO THE KEY THEMES AND ISSUES

Two characters mentioned only passing in the last chapter are Rosencrantz and Guildenstern: secondary figures whose identities are curious for a number of reasons. They too exemplify the basic problem of distinguishing between allies and enemies in *Hamlet*. Although they are two of Hamlet's long-established friends (having been – or perhaps they still are – his 'schoolfellows' (3.4.200), a term which could imply that they are fellow university students too, like Horatio), nevertheless their employment by Claudius indicates a deep complication in their relationship to the Prince, who soon sees them as 'adders fanged' rather than as his 'good lads' (3.4.200–1; 2.2.220). While they fully deserve Hamlet's raw castigation – he stuns Guildenstern into silence with the pithy question, 'Do you think I am easier to be played on than a pipe?' at 3.2.361–2, and mocks Rosencrantz as a 'sponge' that 'soaks up the King's [. . .] rewards' at 4.2.11–15 – whether they merit death, as Hamlet later engineers it, is more questionable. Perhaps Horatio's difficult-to-read response to this news in 5.2 could register an uncertainty on his behalf (and on ours too) about Hamlet's ethical identity. After all, what kind of hero can send his friends so unconcernedly to their deaths, as Hamlet does? 'Am I next?', may well be what Horatio is thinking here (should we wish to speculate about such ineffable things).

More significantly, though, Rosencrantz and Guildenstern are not just difficult to distinguish as friends or foes: they are, crucially and also strangely, difficult to differentiate from each other. That we are meant to notice this peculiar trait is clear, both from the first occasion in which we meet them (when the Queen, as it can be played in performance at least, seems diplomatically to correct the King in mistaking 'gentle Guildenstern' for 'gentle Rosencrantz' and vice versa (2.2.33–4)), and also from the way in which the two characters share the same voice (almost literally) through indistinct styles of talking. In 2.2, they address the King and Queen individually, but nevertheless as a two-in-one entity – speaking as an 'us' and for 'we both' (ll. 27, 29) – while elsewhere the lines of either could be delivered as easily by the one as by the other. They are inseparable too, only ever appearing together in *Hamlet*; and this strange joined-at-the-hip effect is intensified by the fact that, even while talking as one person, they never speak to each other. We can see how a writer like Tom Stoppard would take great delight in making these two strangely interchangeable characters the heroes of their own absurdist existential tragicomedy, *Rosencrantz and Guildenstern are Dead* (1966). Yet the question still remains: what are these two characters doing in *Hamlet*? And why pay two actors to play what is essentially one part? 'Why two salaries?' is Michael Pennington's pragmatic point about this odd couple (182). What is their function, then, as a pair? The aim of this Conclusion is to address these questions as a way of examining not just the roles of Rosencrantz and Guildenstern in *Hamlet*, but of how they illustrate something of the play's key ideas and issues: visually and dramatically, generically and linguistically. Rosencrantz and Guildenstern allow us to see further into how *Hamlet* works as a play. But they also permit us to review Hamlet as a character stranded in a drama haunted by doubles of various kinds – rhetorical, textual, theatrical – amid which he seems to be surrounded by other versions of himself, and yet tragically alone.

AT EACH EAR A HEARER

As with other minor parts in *Hamlet*, the (joint) role played by Rosencrantz and Guildenstern is clear enough in many respects. In their service as the King's spies, they signal something of the corruption of the new regime, which can transform school friends into hirelings with little effort, and which Rosencrantz and Guildenstern come to exemplify as two who 'did make love' to their deadly 'employment', as the Folio *Hamlet* has it (*Hamlet* 1987, 5.2.58). Scuttling crab-like between Claudius and Hamlet (the only characters with whom they properly interact in the play), they are revealed as sycophantic in the company of the King (as in the opening dialogue of 3.3, where they speak formally in verse) and as laddishly bawdy with the Prince (at least in 2.2), with whom they speak as equals, in prose. Aside from their ability to soak up sponge-like the speech habits of those with whom they talk, their exchanges with Hamlet suggest that Rosencrantz and Guildenstern function as another pair of foils for the Prince, whose 'antic disposition' foils every attempt they make to fathom the source of his recent alteration. Like Polonius, then, they serve to reveal the range and depth of Hamlet's wit, as well as the 'savage side to Hamlet' and his 'ruthlessness' (Wilson, 102–3), when evading their invasiveness and in sending them to their deaths in England.

But while Hamlet's scenes with Rosencrantz and Guildenstern give us some brilliant set pieces in the play (such as the prose semi-soliloquy of 2.2, in which Hamlet explains that he has 'of late, but wherefore I know not, lost all my mirth' (2.2.259–76), a confession which seems both recognizably feigned and entirely truthful), they also serve to keep alive the political dimension of Hamlet's grievances as Denmark's 'powerless prince' (Burns, 141). It is with these old friends and good lads that Hamlet cites his lack of 'advancement' as the supposed cause of his recent 'griefs' (3.2.330), a point underscored in the Folio text where, in a passage not found in the Second Quarto version of 2.2, Hamlet puzzles his spies with some quick-shifting talk about how 'Denmark's a prison' because, as Rosencrantz assumes, his 'ambition makes it one' (*Hamlet* 1987, 2.2.238–67). Whether such hints are designed to distract these 'adders' – thrown out to lead them astray, by giving them what they want to hear – is never quite clear. Either way, such sentiments remind us at key moments that Hamlet's story is not just one of personal revenge, but also of political injustice and dispossession. There is some truth perhaps behind such exchanges.

Yet, we must still wonder why Shakespeare has two characters perform this singular dramatic function? The fact that there is no obvious need to have two of Hamlet's 'schoolfellows' to 'pluck out the heart' of his 'mystery' (3.4.200; 3.2.357–8) when one, presumably, might do just as well suggests that the doubleness of Rosencrantz and Guildenstern is in itself dramatically important, contributing to the drama in significant, even emblematic ways. There is something fundamentally menacing, for example, about the way in which Rosencrantz and Guildenstern approach Hamlet always as a duo, as if Hamlet is being outnumbered or pincered in his encounters with them, and so has to be doubly sharp, doubly quick-witted as a result. By moving and talking always in tandem, we get a powerful sense of how sinister this double act might be. We should not underestimate either the sheer *strangeness* that Rosencrantz and Guildenstern lend to *Hamlet*. Everything about them seems to generate unease, from their eerie indistinctness (actors playing them may have to wear different colours to be distinguished, for example) to their seemingly telepathic ability to act and speak together without communicating directly with one another. Naturally, then, these dramatic twins contribute to the claustrophobia of Hamlet's world (which is a 'prison' to him, as he confesses to them in 2.2 of the Folio text), as well as to the dream-like, surreal quality of *Hamlet*, as they stalk the Prince in unison, as in some through-the-looking-glass nightmare. As much as the Ghost's terrifying appearance or Ophelia's bizarrely beautiful drowning, Rosencrantz and Guildenstern inform our sense that *Hamlet* is a play full of 'bad dreams' (*Hamlet* 1987, 2.2.253–4).

The visual function of Rosencrantz and Guildenstern is perhaps most important to register. When Polonius is about to re-enter 2.2, for example, Hamlet directs his 'good lads' to stand beside him, 'at each ear a hearer' (2.2.318–19). While this implied stage direction (easy enough to overlook) underscores Hamlet's awareness of them both as spies and eavesdroppers – 'hearers' as well as observers for Claudius – this balancing of one on either side of him offers us a telling arrangement. It may remind us, for instance, of the roles played by the 'Good' and 'Bad' angels of Christopher Marlowe's *Dr Faustus*, who may be imagined advising Faustus standing at each ear, generating doubts about the binary choices available to him: whether to continue in sin or to repent, for instance, with Faustus unsure which to follow (A-text, 1.1.72–9; 2.1.15–21; 2.3.12–17). Just such radical uncertainty is articulated by the speaker of Shakespeare's sonnet 144 (first published in 1599, in *The Passionate Pilgrim*), who is likewise trapped in a nightmarish love triangle created by his 'better angel' and a 'worser spirit', while caught in the 'hell' of his unproven suspicions that something is going on between them (*Shakespeare's Sonnets* 1997, 1–6, 402–4). As a visual arrangement, standing 'at each ear' reminds us of how so many relationships in *Hamlet* (as we saw in the last chapter) are triangular in nature, often leaving Hamlet caught between two alternatives: between Gertrude and Ophelia, or Ophelia and Laertes, or Laertes and

Fortinbras, or Fortinbras and the Ghost, or the Ghost and Claudius, or Claudius and Gertrude, and so on. On this basis too, Rosencrantz and Guildenstern could be seen as an emblem of all the dualities and doubles that haunt *Hamlet* as a drama. They become a life-size embodiment of a pattern evident throughout the play, whereby our attention is drawn to objects, persons, and images that are simultaneously distinct and yet difficult to distinguish: uncles and fathers, cousins and sons, mothers and lovers, Hyperions and satyrs, hawks and handsaws, spirits and goblins, pickers and stealers, accidents, murders and suicides. When Horatio describes the Ghost to Hamlet in 1.2 as being 'like your father' he makes his point both visually and emphatically: 'These hands are not more like', he says (1.2.211). Much the same could be said of Rosencrantz and Guildenstern.

We might conclude that when it comes to communicating the play's recurring fascination with issues of identity and of self, this pair plays an important role. Yet there is more to it than this. Rosencrantz and Guildenstern also provide a sort of visual *coda* for *Hamlet*'s rhetorical structuring around an all-pervasive language of doubles and doublings. As a couple, for instance, Rosencrantz and Guildenstern seem to embody the regime-defining language of balance and antithesis used by Claudius in the public speeches of 1.2 to justify his uneasy union to his 'sometime sister'. Their very names seem to balance across the same hinges of Claudius's opening rhetoric of 'green' and 'grief', 'sister' and 'Queen', 'mirth' and 'dirge' – and so too Rose'n'crantz and Guild'n'stern. But as characters they also mirror visually and physically the play's recurring use of the 'one-through-two' figure of speech known as *hendiadys*, where two words are coupled to serve in the place of one (being joined in the middle by 'and'), and which dominates the language patterns of *Hamlet* in a way unique among Shakespeare's dramatic works, bequeathing to it a 'perception of doubleness in everything' (Wright 177; see also Palfrey, 39–57). Hendiadys can be seen (and heard), for example, in the Prince's '*book and volume* of my brain' (1.5.103), and in his call to '*Angels and ministers* of grace' to defend him (1.4.39), or in Horatio's description of Hamlet's '*wild and whirling* words' (1.5.132). As George T. Wright has shown, it is hardly a linguistic trait limited to Hamlet either, who nevertheless has an extra habit of doubling what he says through repetition, as in 'My tables! My tables!' and 'Very like, very like' (*Hamlet* 1987, 1.5.107–8; 1.2.238), though more so in the Folio text (Bradley, 125). As with all the other rhetorical couplings in the play, from Hamlet's opening quip on 'kin' and 'kind' (1.2.65) to the most famous antithesis in the English language – 'To be, or not to be' (3.1.55) – Shakespeare's deployment of hendiadys in *Hamlet* seems designed to disturb and complicate perceptions both in and of the play's action. As Wright puts it: 'hendiadys, far from explaining mysteries, establishes them' in *Hamlet*, primarily because it offers 'not merely amplification or intensification' as a rhetorical device, 'but an interweaving, sometimes a muddling of meanings', thereby revealing how 'dualisms' tend to be 'misleading' in the play and 'unions to be false or unsteady' (169, 173, 178). In this way, all of *Hamlet*'s rhetorical doublings – from oxymoron and antithesis to hendiadys and the simple pun – offer a 'stylistic means of underlining the play's themes of anxiety, bafflement, disjunction, and the falsity of appearances' (Wright, 178). Rosencrantz and Guildenstern are the visible component of this 'anxiety, bafflement, disjunction' in *Hamlet*. They are a visual hendiadys, a physical 'one-through-two': a duo impossible to separate and between whom it becomes difficult to distinguish true from false, friend from foe, reality from representation. To borrow Wright's description of hendiadys's dizzying effects in *Hamlet*, Rosencrantz and Guildenstern are 'mirrors' that distort 'the reality they pretend to reproduce', and whose *unheimlich* togetherness (like Claudius's marriage to his 'sometime sister') 'mocks normal unions of entities' (Wright, 181). This odd couple stand, then, neither in the margins of *Hamlet*'s structures of meaning nor at the periphery of our experience of the play: they remain at the core of both.

TRAGICALLY . . . AN ONLY TWIN

Although there is nothing at all to suggest that Rosencrantz and Guildenstern are brothers, they nevertheless appear to us as dramatic twins, whose names, faces, and speaking parts are quite interchangeable. As such, they could be seen as emblematic of the play's propensity to generate other kinds of twins, not just in the rhetorical figures and tropes that characterize the drama's language at almost every level, but in the way the plot twins names and destinies (of young and old Hamlet, and young and old Fortinbras, for example), as well as roles (with Hamlet and Laertes as revengers, Hamlet and Polonius as fools, Hamlet and the gravediggers – two of them, naturally – as clowns, and so on). We could even see this drive towards doubles extending beyond the play, as it characterizes the textual history of *Hamlet*: a drama for which there are two near identical – but also significantly different – early printed versions (the Second Quarto and the First Folio texts, not to mention the valuable First Quarto *Hamlet*), and which is haunted by another no longer extant revenge tragedy, also called *Hamlet*, on which Shakespeare's play is probably based. *Hamlet* thus comes to us as an echo of another *Hamlet*, and so remains one of an original pair, an only twin, or a fatherless play, with the parent drama remaining a ghostly presence hovering around Shakespeare's later reinvention of it (or so the story might go).

Rosencrantz and Guildenstern are very much of a piece with *Hamlet* for all these reasons. Yet as twins (of a sort) they also remind us how deliberately, as a tragedy, *Hamlet* slips into another dramatic identity (its generic twin, so to speak) on various occasions: that of comedy. The place we are most likely to find two characters who are practically indistinguishable from one another in face and voice (if this is how we imagine Rosencrantz and Guildenstern) is not a Senecan revenge tragedy such as *Hamlet*, but an 'errors' play such as Shakespeare's *The Comedy of Errors* or *Twelfth Night* (both indebted to the Roman comedy *Menaechmi*, by Plautus), the plotting of which works primarily through the farcical confusion and madness generated by having two characters (or four, as is the case in *The Comedy of Errors*) who look and sound identical. In this respect, Rosencrantz and Guildenstern seem to have stepped into the wrong kind of play. As Robert Miola puts it, 'Clones and identical twins unsettle and amuse' primarily because the 'doubling of one's face, so basic and private a marker of self, disables any pretension to dignity, individuality, and importance': the 'comic possibilities' afforded by such 'doubling' are, then, obvious (Miola, 73). Rosencrantz and Guildenstern are far from identical, of course. But they have something of a similar effect, drawing our attention to issues of identity and individuality, and adding to our sense of *Hamlet* as a distorted comedy, in which other characters too have their stock comical roles twisted into tragic forms: Polonius as the *senex* (old man), Ophelia as the *virgo* (marriageable girl), and both Hamlet and Laertes as versions of the *adulescens* (young man) (Miola, 72). We might think of *Hamlet*, then, as a play that cannot make up its mind, being (to rephrase Polonius's formulation) at once too 'heavy' for Plautus and his comedies, and too 'light' for Seneca and his tragedies (2.2.336–7), yet somehow mixing elements from both.

Hamlet could be read, therefore, as the counterpart in tragedy to the comedy of *Twelfth Night*, a play probably written in close proximity to *Hamlet*: around 1601, and so 'either immediately before or straight after *Hamlet*', as its Oxford editors suggest (1994, 1). *Hamlet* certainly shares with this comedy a number of its key issues and concerns: the exploration of identity and the 'self', for instance, as well as of madness and mistakes, jesters and farce, marriages and mourning, homosocial bonds and family ties, friendships and deceptions, behind all of which in *Twelfth Night* stand the twinned plots of separated twins and of the 'revenges' that the 'whirligig of time' brings about. While the licensed fool of *Twelfth Night*, Feste, whose profession Viola admires as 'a practice / As full of labour as a wise man's art' (3.1.64–5), gives to us a twin of the 'antic' Hamlet, nevertheless the connections between *Hamlet* and the kind of 'errors' comedy to which Shakespeare returned when writing *Twelfth Night* (a twin of *The Comedy of Errors*, which twins in turn Plautus's *Menaechmi*) are perhaps yet more significant. Robert Miola certainly sees *Hamlet* as 'Shakespeare's culminating encounter with Plautus' *Menaechmi*', in the way it re-works the basic elements of this type of play. Like the heroes of such comedies, Hamlet also 'wanders through a strange yet familiar world', meeting 'friends, family, and lovers' who 'are not who they claim to be; nor is he himself', having so many different identities to assume and so many roles to play. Because 'Hamlet suffers a tragic version of errors-play *aporia*, a deep confusion about himself and the world', then it seems that in *Hamlet* Shakespeare 'raises to a higher level' questions 'about identity and the nature of illusion and the self in the world', explored and examined and reworked in Plautine comedies like *Twelfth Night* (Miola, 80–1; Levin, 119–20).

All of this can help us to see Hamlet's character (and *Hamlet*'s characters) differently. As we explored in Chapter 3, *Hamlet* appears to be full of doubles with whom Shakespeare twins his Prince in complex dramatic and rhetorical ways. Yet despite the vertiginous number of simulacra we have of Hamlet (in the Ghost, in Claudius, in Polonius, in Laertes, in Horatio), key to Hamlet's tragedy is his *singularity* (see Levin, 52–3, 67). Whereas *The Comedy of Errors* and *Twelfth Night* resolve their confusions through the final, wondrous moment of reunion, where (as if by some miracle) the twins meet again, leaving the other on-stage characters to undergo an epiphany of realization and understanding, no such ending is available to Hamlet: no such clarity is released. When Hamlet does meet his twin, his recognition scene is transformed into something both poignant yet macabre, occurring in the graveyard of 5.1 where Hamlet is suddenly reunited with his last double – the dead fool, Yorick – whose skull he contemplates as if it were a mirror filled with his own dark reflections. Hamlet's words signal complex, twinned emotions at this point, of wonder and of nostalgia but also of disgust, as he declares, 'I knew him, Horatio. A / fellow of infinite jest, of most excellent fancy', before casting aside this reeking *memento mori* with no more than a 'Pah!' (5.1.174–5, 190). Perhaps what makes this moment with Yorick's skull so memorable, and so profound, is the same moving and unsettling quality which characterizes *Hamlet* as a tragedy. For what we engage with in *Hamlet* is the existential loneliness of a long-standing joke: of a man who remains, tragically, an only twin.

NOTES

INTRODUCTION: AN OVERVIEW OF *HAMLET*

1 For Jonson's famous comment on Shakespeare's Latin and Greek see his dedicatory poem 'To the Memory of My Beloved, the Author, Mr William Shakespeare', first published in the First Folio of Shakespeare's *Comedies, Histories, and Tragedies* (1623), in Jonson 1996, 263–5, and Vickers 2003, 537–40.

2 For Jonson's other comments on Shakespeare, see Vickers 2003, 532, 561–62; Jonson 1985, 539–40, 599. See also 'The Induction on the Stage' in *Bartholomew Fair* (Jonson 1960, 6–13).

3 On literary ideas of rhetorical and dramatic decorum in the Renaissance, and in relation to *Hamlet*, see McAlindon 1973, 1–18, 44–79.

4 See Vickers 1981; Bligh; Lee, 95–145; Desmet 1992, 35–58; de Grazia 2007, 7–22, 158–204; Conklin, 44–81.

5 Pope's comments on Shakespeare's characters being 'Copies' of 'Nature her self' can be found in the preface to his 1725 edition of *The Works of Shakespeare*, in Vickers 1974–81, vol. 2, 403–18, and cited by Lee, 109–10. For Johnson's praise of Shakespeare as a 'poet of nature', especially in the construction of 'characters' as 'the genuine progeny of humanity' see the 'Preface' to his 1765 edition of Shakespeare's plays, in Johnson, 120–65 (122).

6 For other psychoanalytic readings of *Hamlet*, see also Jones 1949; Lacan; Kerrigan 1994; Armstrong. See also Adelman.

7 For other studies and readings of Hamlet as a sufferer of melancholy see Wilson, 116–18, 226–8; Lyons 1971; States, 63–86.

8 For Harold Bloom, this aspect of Shakespeare's art – the 'latency' of his characters as 'real' persons (Nuttall 2007, 173, and Nuttall 1984, 18–31) – explains why his works have a lasting, universal quality, constituting the 'canonical sublime' (Bloom 1999, 428). Lorna Hutson has shown that early modern audiences would have been expected, in a judicial and legal context, to read and to judge theatrical 'character' by inference too (see Hutson 2002; 2005).

9 Unless otherwise indicated, all subsequent quotations from *Hamlet* refer to this edition. See also the 'Note on the edition used' at the end of this chapter.

10 Seneca 1982, 2.20–1. This line (in Latin) is also quoted in Marston 1978, 3.2.51, and is cited by Mercer, 26; Miola, 117; de Grazia 2007, 191–2.

11 The textual history of *Hamlet* and its variants (Q1 1603, Q2 1604/05, and Folio 1623) is accounted fully in the introductory material, notes and appendices to most scholarly editions of the play, such as *Hamlet* 1982; *Hamlet* 1985; *Hamlet* 1987; *Hamlet* 2006a and 2006b. Key assessments of *Hamlet*'s texts are available in the essays and studies listed in the Bibliography and Further Reading. See especially Urkowitz; Werstine (1988); Erlich; Marcus, 132–76; Lee, 228–39; Foakes 1993, 88–97.

12 On these issues, and how they affect our reading of 'character, see de Grazia and Stallybrass 1993; McLoud 1991; Stallybrass 2000.

13 Grady, 24–5. On de Montaigne's ideas of 'self' and their relation to Shakespeare and Shakespearean character formation, see Ellrodt; Davis; Grady.

1. THE MAN IN BLACK: MEETING PRINCE HAMLET

1 Hamlet's 'flesh' in the first soliloquy (1.2.129) presents a famous editorial problem. In the two Quarto versions of *Hamlet* (of 1603 and 1604/05), it is described as 'sallied flesh', suggesting 'assailed, besieged' (*Hamlet* 2006a, 175, n.129), whereas in the 1623 Folio text it is given as 'solid flesh' (*Hamlet* 1987, and see Hibbard's editorial note, 382–4). Some editors have tried to solve the problem by adopting a new word unknown to any of the originally printed texts – 'sullied' (in, for example, *Hamlet* 1936, and *Hamlet* 1980).

2 Compare the last soliloquy in *Doctor Faustus* (A-text), 5.2.65–123: here Faustus cries 'O God' and desires to be 'dissolved in elements' (l. 111) rather than to continue to exist in damnation.

3 On the issue of 'incest' in *Hamlet*, in relation to Claudius's and Gertrude's marriage that is, see Rosenblatt; Frye, 76–82; McCabe; Jardine 1996, 35–47.

4 On Hamlet's potential identity as a 'Protestant' figure, see Matheson; Hassel; Waddington. See also Rust.

2. HERO, VILLAIN, FOOL: THE CHARACTER OF HAMLET'S REVENGE

1 Gabriel Harvey (1966), *Foure Letters and Certeine Sonnets, especially touching Robert Greene and other Parties by him Abused*. Orig. pub 1592. Ed. G.B. Harrison. Edinburgh, 40, 19; and cited in Greene 2007, xiii. I owe thanks to Dr Nandini Das for drawing my attention to this description of Greene as an *omnigatherum*. In his *Groatsworth of Wit* (1592), Robert Greene famously offers one of the earliest descriptions of

Shakespeare to appear in print, complaining about him as an 'upstart crow' and 'an absolute *Johannes fac totem*' (jack-of-all-trades) (Bate 1997, 14–16).

2 This point has been gleaned from Nicholl 2004, 285–6, citing Freud (2000), *Leonardo da Vinci: A Memory of His Childhood*. Trans. Alan Dyson. Orig. pub. 1910. London, 75–6.

3 The Chorus is a feature of Classical drama especially. Both Kyd's *The Spanish Tragedy* and Marlowe's *Dr Faustus* include a Chorus, as does Shakespeare's *Romeo and Juliet*, and more extensively *Henry V* and *Pericles*. The part of 'Time' in *The Winter's Tale* serves as a Chorus of sorts: its speech bridges the gap of 16 years that divides the play's action and its locations. On Shakespeare's use of the Chorus see for example Brennan; Danson; Palmer; Bruster and Weimann.

4 On the history of editing *Hamlet*, see the introductions to *Hamlet* 1985; *Hamlet* 1987; *Hamlet* 2006a; Walsh, 111–98; Mowat 1988; Marcus.

3. FAMILIES, FRIENDS, ENEMIES: *HAMLET*'S OTHER CHARACTERS

1 See especially Jardine 1983, 92–3; Jardine 1996, 35–47; de Grazia 2007, 81–128.

2 The use of a bed in the performance of the 'closet scene' (turning it into a 'bedroom scene') seems to be a twentieth-century staging innovation, designed to underscore an Oedipal interpretation of *Hamlet* (see *Hamlet* 1999, 209; and Dawson). On the early modern 'closet' as a private, intimate space, 'where customarily a woman would only entertain her husband or lover', see Jardine 1996, 148–52 (151). On Gertrude and sexuality see also Jardine 1983, 92–3; Rose; Adelman, 11–37; Ouditt.

3 On the Ghost's theological identity and its relationship to Catholicism and the doctrine of Purgatory, see especially Battenhouse; West; Frye, 14–29; McGee, 43–74; Low; Greenblatt 2000; Freeman.

FURTHER READING

This annotated list of selected editions, essays and studies offers guidance to just *a few* of the works available in a rich and ever-expanding field of literary research. It should be supplemented by further reference to the Bibliography.

PRIMARY TEXTS

Bertram, P and B. W. Kliman (eds) (1991), *The Three-Text Hamlet: Parallel Texts of the First and Second Quartos and First Folio*. New York: AMS Press. A great resource. This edition allows readers to examine all three early printed texts of *Hamlet* (1603, 1604/05, and 1623) side-by-side, line-by-line, thus making their textual differences easy to see.

Hansen, William F. (1983), *Saxo Grammaticus and the Life of Hamlet: A Translation, History, and Commentary*. Lincoln, Nebraska and London: University of Nebraska Press. A very useful translation of the Danish legend of Amleth. The introduction discusses its possible relationship as a narrative to Shakespeare's play. A helpful supplement to the sources and analogues collected in Bullough, vol. 7.

Shakespeare, William (1982) *Hamlet*. Ed. H. Jenkins. London: Arden Shakespeare/Methuen. Although superseded by the latest Arden edition of *Hamlet* (2006a), this is still a valuable resource with an excellent introduction, notes and critical materials. The text is a conflation of the play's textual variants.

Shakespeare, William (1985) *Hamlet*. Ed. P. Edwards. Cambridge: Cambridge University Press. Another valuable scholarly edition, with an excellent introduction. Although a collated version, the Second Quarto's textual variants are helpfully signalled in this edition by square brackets.

Shakespeare, William (1987) *Hamlet*. Ed. G.R. Hibbard. Oxford: Oxford University Press. An edition based on the Folio text (1623), with the Second Quarto's substantial variants usefully included in an appendix. Excellent introduction and prefatory materials.

Shakespeare, William (1999) *Hamlet*. Ed. R. Hapgood. Cambridge: Cambridge University Press. A performance history edition, with notes illustrating how lines, speeches and scenes have been performed on stage over the last 400 years, and on screen too (including details of costume and stage design). The introduction is excellent, giving an overview of the history of *Hamlet* in performance.

Shakespeare, William (2006a) *Hamlet*. Ed. A. Thompson and N. Taylor. London: Arden Shakespeare/Thomson Learning. An edition based on the Second Quarto text (1604/05), and so a valuable alternative to Hibbard's Folio-based edition (*Hamlet* 1987). Includes an appendix giving those passages found only in the Folio text. Excellent introduction, notes and other critical materials.

Shakespeare, William (2006b) *Hamlet: The Texts of 1603 and 1623*. Ed. A. Thompson and N. Taylor. London: Arden Shakespeare/Thomson Learning. A great resource, publishing the First Quarto (1603) and First Folio (1623) texts together in one volume. A valuable companion to the latest Arden edition of *Hamlet* (2006a). Excellent notes and critical material.

SECONDARY TEXTS

Armstrong, Philip (2001) *Shakespeare in Psychoanalysis*. London and New York: Routledge/Taylor & Francis. An excellent, informative account of psychoanalytic readings of Shakespeare's plays, with a particular focus on *Hamlet*, Freud and Lacan. This book makes accessible Freudian and Lacanian approaches to the play, and illustrates how valuable they can be.

Bate, Jonathan (ed.) (1992) *The Romantics on Shakespeare*. Harmondsworth: Penguin. A compendium of commentary and criticism of Shakespeare from the late eighteenth and early nineteenth centuries. This anthology includes the key statements on *Hamlet* by Romantic writers, such as Goethe, Coleridge, Hazlitt, and many others.

Bloom, Harold (1995) *The Western Canon: The Books and School of the Ages*. Basingstoke: Macmillan. A provocative and engaging examination of Western literature's 'great books'. Bloom places Shakespeare (and especially *Hamlet*) at the centre of the 'Western canon'.

Booth, Stephen (1969) 'On the value of *Hamlet*' in Rabkin, N. (ed.), *Reinterpreting Elizabethan Drama*. New York and London: Columbia University Press, 137–76. A valuable essay. Booth addresses how *Hamlet* is structured and how we experience it as readers and audiences.

Bradley, A.C. (1992) *Shakespearean Tragedy*. 3rd edn. Basingstoke: Macmillan. Though often maligned and considered old-fashioned, Bradley's discussions of *Hamlet* are often sharp and insightful. His readings of the play keep an eye on what is happening on the stage as much as on the page (or in the characters themselves). John Russell Brown's excellent introduction makes clear how Bradley's commentary remains important.

Burns, Edward (1990) *Character: Acting and Being on the Pre-Modern Stage*. Basingstoke, Macmillan. An excellent study of the idea of dramatic 'character', from Aristotle and Classical drama to early modern and contemporary theatre.

Conklin, Paul S. (1947) *A History of Hamlet Criticism 1601–1821*. London: Routledge & Kegan Paul. A useful overview of the critical responses to and debates over *Hamlet* from the 1600s to the early nineteenth century.

Coyle, Martin (ed.) (1992) *Hamlet: New Casebook*. Basingstoke: Palgrave. A collection that helpfully reprints some key essays and studies of *Hamlet* published in the second half of the twentieth century. It includes those essays on the play (cited in the Bibliography) by Booth, Edwards, Showalter and Smith, along with extracts from Belsey, and others.

Dawson, Anthony (1995) *Shakespeare in Performance: Hamlet*. Manchester: Manchester University Press. An excellent account of the history of *Hamlet* in performance. Includes a wealth of helpful information about how the play was adapted for stage and screen from the 1600s and the Restoration onwards, through the eighteenth and nineteenth centuries to the 1990s.

de Grazia, Margreta (2007) *Hamlet Without Hamlet*. Cambridge: Cambridge University Press. A stimulating and helpful book, illuminating some of *Hamlet*'s historical and interpretative contexts. de Grazia examines the emergence of Hamlet as a 'modern' or 'psychological' character, among other issues.

Eliot, T.S. (1928) 'Hamlet and his problems' in *The Sacred Wood: Essays on Poetry and Criticism*. 2nd edn. London: Methuen, 95–103. A short but important – because provocative – essay which regards *Hamlet* as an artistic failure, and which applies the idea of the 'objective correlative' to Hamlet's character and to his relationship with Gertrude. Useful to consider alongside the readings of Freud, Jones (1949), Lacan and Adelman.

Foakes, R.A. (1993) *Hamlet Versus Lear: Cultural Politics and Shakespeare's Art*. Cambridge: Cambridge University Press. An engaging examination of the place of *Hamlet* and *King Lear* in twentieth-century Western culture. Offers valuable discussions of *Hamlet* as a play and as a source of literary and cultural influence. Foakes also offers a spirited defence of the aesthetic value of Shakespearean drama.

Frye, Roland Mushat (1984) *The Renaissance Hamlet: Issues and Responses in 1600*. Princeton, NJ: Princeton University Press. An encyclopaedic compendium of information on *Hamlet* in its own time. Frye provides detailed discussions of everything from early modern religious attitudes (Catholic and Protestant), to the doctrine of Purgatory, to the funeral rites of Ophelia, and the significance of Yorick's skull in relation to Renaissance art and literature.

Gurr, Andrew and Mariko Ichikawa (2000) *Staging in Shakespeare's Theatres*. Oxford: Oxford University Press. A useful introduction to the staging practices of early modern English theatres: it includes an illustrative chapter on 'The early staging of *Hamlet*'.

Holmes, Jonathan (2004) *Merely Players? Actors Accounts of Performing Shakespeare*. London and New York: Routledge/Taylor & Francis. An excellent survey and analysis of actors' accounts of playing Shakespearean roles. This book has much to say on character-formation from the perspective of the players. Holmes draws on actors' experiences to address the theatrical traditions that contribute to Shakespearean parts and how character is performed.

Jackson, Russell (ed.) (2000) *The Cambridge Companion to Shakespeare on Film*. Cambridge: Cambridge University Press. A useful volume which includes chapters on individual directors (Olivier, Kozintzev, Zeffirelli, and Branagh), all of whom have adapted *Hamlet* for the cinema, along with essays on Hamlet and film specifically. Bibliographically useful for further reading on Shakespeare and film.

Johnson, Samuel (1989) *Samuel Johnson on Shakespeare*. Ed. W.R. Woodhuysen. Harmondsworth: Penguin. A good anthology of Johnson's writings on Shakespeare. It includes the full 'Preface' to Johnson's 1765 edition of Shakespeare's plays (an important work of criticism in itself), along with selected notes by Johnson on individual plays' characters, lines and scenes.

Jump, John (ed.) (1968) *Hamlet: A Casebook*. London: Macmillan. This is still a useful anthology of criticism, collecting comments on the play from the early eighteenth century to the mid-twentieth century, and reprinting essays and extracts from studies (cited in the Bibliography) by Bradley, Eliot, Jones (1949), Levin and Kott.

Kliman, Bernice W. (1988) *Hamlet: Film, Television, and Audio Performance*. London and Toronto: Associated University Presses. A detailed study of *Hamlet* and its twentieth-century performances on screen. Includes chapters on Olivier's (1948), Kozintzev's (1964) and Richardson's (1969) film adaptations.

Lee, John (2000) *Shakespeare's Hamlet and the Controversies of Self*. Oxford: Clarendon Press. An encyclopaedic assessment of critical approaches to 'character', 'self' and 'subjectivity' in *Hamlet*, from Montaigne and Hazlitt to the contemporary quarrels of New Historicist and Cultural Materialist criticism.

Levin, Harry (1959) *The Question of Hamlet*. New York: Oxford University Press. This is still a valuable study. Levin reads the play carefully through its 'interrogative' moods and modes, focusing on doubt, irony and questioning as central to its dramatic structures and principles.

Mercer, Peter (1987) *Hamlet and the Acting of Revenge*. Basingstoke, Macmillan. A detailed reading of *Hamlet* as a revenge tragedy. Mercer considers the play in relation to the traditions – Classical and Renaissance – of the genre, and illustrates the ways in which Shakespeare both follows these traditions, but also redefines them in *Hamlet*.

Mills, John A. (1985) *Hamlet on Stage: The Great Tradition*. London: Greenwood Press. A useful compilation of (and commentary upon) actors' performances of the part of Hamlet on stage, from Richard Burbage to Richard Burton.

Palfrey, Simon (2005) *Doing Shakespeare*. London: Arden Shakespeare/ Thomson Learning. An excellent book on reading Shakespeare's active art as a poet-dramatist: it includes very useful discussions of 'character' and its relationship to the idea of the actor's 'part', as well as of soliloquy and hendiadys.

Pennington, Michael (1996) *Hamlet: A User's Guide*. London: Nick Hern Books. Having played most of the roles in *Hamlet* throughout his career as an actor, this book offers a range of important insights into the play, both on the page and in performance. Pennington is a sensitive reader of the text, and an engaging writer too, making this one of the most useful and accessible books on *Hamlet* available. Pennington addresses the play Act-by-Act, and includes a section dedicated to the 'characters' of *Hamlet*.

Rothwell, Kenneth S. (2004) *A History of Shakespeare on Screen: A Century of Film and Television*. 2nd edn. Cambridge: Cambridge University Press. A great survey of Shakespeare on screen, offering pithy summaries of (and some critical commentary upon) the films of the plays. Very useful for the history of *Hamlet* on screen.

States, Bert O. (1992) *Hamlet and the Concept of Character*. Baltimore and London: Johns Hopkins University Press. A book-length study of *Hamlet* and 'character' that offers some useful and valuable points and ideas, and in many ways goes against the grain of recent critical thinking about Shakespearean 'character'. Includes sections addressing the 'concept' of 'character' more broadly, as well as the individual characters of *Hamlet*.

Thomson, Peter (1992) *Shakespeare's Theatre*. 2nd edn. London: Routledge. A useful introduction to the early modern stage and its practices: includes a chapter on '*Hamlet* and the actor in Shakespeare's theatre'.

Urkowitz, Steven (1986) ' "Well-sayd olde mole": burying three *Hamlets* in modern editions' in G. Ziegler (ed.), *Shakespeare Study Today*. New York: AMS Press, 37–70. A key essay in the status of *Hamlet* and its variant texts in relation to modern editing practices.

Walsh, Marcus (1997) *Shakespeare, Milton, and Eighteenth-Century Literary Editing*. Cambridge: Cambridge University Press. This book offers an excellent, detailed account of the modern editing of Shakespeare in the eighteenth century (by Lewis Theobald and others).

Werstine, Paul (1988) 'The textual mystery of *Hamlet*', *Shakespeare Quarterly*, 39, 1–26. Another key essay on *Hamlet* and its variant texts, and their implications for our readings of the play.

Wilson, John Dover (1951) *What Happens in Hamlet*. 3rd edn. Cambridge: Cambridge University Press. Although idiosyncratic in style and approach, this is still a very useful book-length study of *Hamlet*. Its strengths lie in its attention to detail, and in that fact that Wilson approaches the play from a number of perspectives, especially as an editor of the text, and as one sensitive to the how the play works in performance.

BIBLIOGRAPHY

PRIMARY TEXTS

Aristotle (1968), *Poetics*. Trans. Leon Golden. Englewood Cliffs, NJ: Prentice-Hall.

Bertram, P and B.W. Kliman (eds) (1991) *The Three-Text Hamlet: Parallel Texts of the First and Second Quartos and First Folio*. New York: AMS Press.

Branagh, Kenneth (1996) *Hamlet: Screenplay*. London: Chatto & Windus.

Bullough, Geoffrey (1957–75) *Narrative and Dramatic Sources of Shakespeare*. 8 vols. London: Routledge & Kegan Paul.

Chapman, George, Ben Jonson and John Marston (1979) *Eastward Ho*. Ed. R.W. Van Fossen. Manchester: Manchester University Press.

Cooper, Anthony Ashley, Earl of Shaftesbury (1999) *Characteristics of Men, Manners, Opinions, Times*. Ed. Lawrence E. Klein. Cambridge: Cambridge University Press.

de Montaigne, Michel (1993) *The Complete Essays*. Trans. M.A. Screech. New edn. Harmondsworth: Penguin.

Dent, Alan (ed.) (1948) *Hamlet: The Film and the Play*. London: World Film Publications.

Greene, Robert (2007) *Planetomachia (1585)*. Ed. Nandini Das. Aldershot: Ashgate.

Hall, Joseph (1608) *Characters of Vertues and Vices*. London. Printed by Melch. Bradwood for Eleazor Edgar and Samuel Macham.

Hansen, William F. (1983) *Saxo Grammaticus and the Life of Hamlet: A Translation, History, and Commentary*. Lincoln, Nebraska and London: University of Nebraska Press.

Jonson, Ben (1960) *Bartholomew Fair*. Ed. E.A. Horsman. Manchester: Manchester University Press.

Jonson, Ben (1967) *The Alchemist*. Ed. F.H. Mares. Manchester: Manchester University Press.

Jonson, Ben (1984) *The New Inn*. Ed. Michael Hattaway. Manchester: Manchester University Press.

Jonson, Ben (1985) *Major Works*. Ed. Ian Donaldson. Oxford: Oxford University Press.

Jonson, Ben (1996) *The Complete Poems*. Ed. George Parfitt. Harmondsworth: Penguin.

Jonson, Ben (1999) *Volpone, or The Fox*. Ed. Brian Parker. Rev. edn. Manchester: Manchester University Press.

Jonson, Ben (2000) *Every Man In His Humour*. Ed. Robert S. Miola. Manchester: Manchester University Press.

Kyd, Thomas (1959) *The Spanish Tragedy*. Ed. P. Edwards. London: Methuen.

Marlowe, Christopher (1993) *Doctor Faustus: A- and B-Texts*. Ed. D. Bevington and E. Rasmussen. Manchester: Manchester University Press.

Marston, John (1978) *Antonio's Revenge*. Ed. W. Reavley Gair. Manchester: Manchester University Press.

Murray, P. (ed.) (2000) *Classical Literary Criticism*. Harmondsworth: Penguin.

Overbury, Sir Thomas (attrib.) (1615) *New and Choice Characters, of Severall Authors*. Enlarged edn. London. Printed by Thomas Creede for Lawrence Lisle.

Paylor, W.J. (ed.) (1936) *The Overburian Characters*. Percy Reprints XIII. Oxford, Blackwell.

Russell, D.A. and M. Winterbottom (eds) (1972) *Ancient Literary Criticism*. Oxford: Clarendon Press.

Russell, D.A. and M. Winterbottom (eds) (1998) *Classical Literary Criticism*. Oxford: Oxford University Press.

Seneca, Lucius Annaeus (1966) *Four Tragedies*. Trans. E.F. Watling. Harmondsworth: Penguin.

Seneca, Lucius Annaeus (1982) *Thyestes*. Trans. Jasper Heywood (1560). Ed. Joost Daalder. London: Ernest Benn/New York: W.W. Norton.

Shakespeare, William (1936) *Hamlet*. Ed. John Dover Wilson. 2nd edn. Cambridge: Cambridge University Press.

Shakespeare, William (1980) *Hamlet*. Ed. T.J.B. Spencer. Harmondsworth: Penguin.

Shakespeare, William (1982) *Hamlet*. Ed. H. Jenkins. London: Arden Shakespeare/Methuen.

Shakespeare, William (1985) *Hamlet*. Ed. P. Edwards. Cambridge: Cambridge University Press.

Shakespeare, William (1987) *Hamlet*. Ed. G.R. Hibbard. Oxford: Oxford University Press.

Shakespeare, William (1994) *Twelfth Night*. Ed. Roger Warren and Stanley Wells. Oxford: Oxford University Press.

Shakespeare, William (1997) *Shakespeare's Sonnets*. Ed. K. Duncan-Jones. London: Arden Shakespeare/Thomson Nelson.

Shakespeare, William (1998) *The First Quarto of Hamlet*. Ed. K.O. Irace. Cambridge: Cambridge University Press.

Shakespeare, William (1999) *Hamlet*. Ed. R. Hapgood. Cambridge: Cambridge University Press.

Shakespeare, William (2002) *King Richard II*. Ed. Charles R. Forker. London: Arden Shakespeare/Thomson Learning.

Shakespeare, William (2005) *Complete Works*. Ed. S. Wells, G. Taylor, J. Jowett and W. Montgomery. 2nd edn. Oxford: Oxford University Press.

Shakespeare, William (2006a) *Hamlet*. Ed. A. Thompson and N. Taylor. London: Arden Shakespeare/Thomson Learning.

Shakespeare, William (2006b) *Hamlet: The Texts of 1603 and 1623*. Ed. A. Thompson and N. Taylor. London: Arden Shakespeare/Thomson Learning.

Stoppard, Tom (1978) *Rosencrantz and Guildenstern Are Dead*. London: Faber and Faber.

Sidney, Sir Philip (2002) *An Apology for Poetry*. Ed. R.W. Maslen. 3rd edn. Manchester: Manchester University Press.

Vickers, Brian (ed.) (2003) *English Renaissance Literary Criticism*. Oxford: Oxford University Press.

SECONDARY TEXTS

Aasand, Hardin L. (ed.) (2003) *Stage Directions in Hamlet*. London: Associated University Presses.

Adelman, Janet (1992) *Suffocating Mothers: Fantasies of Maternal Origin in Shakespeare's Plays, Hamlet to The Tempest*. London and New York: Routledge.

Armstrong, Philip (2001) *Shakespeare in Psychoanalysis*. London and New York: Routledge/Taylor & Francis.

Barker, Francis (1995) *The Tremulous Private Body: Essays on Subjection*. 2nd edn. Ann Arbor: University of Michigan Press.

Barroll, J. Leeds (1974) *Artificial Persons: The Formation of Character in the Tragedies of Shakespeare*. Columbia, South Carolina: University of South Carolina.

Bate, Jonathan (1989) *Shakespeare and the English Romantic Imagination*. Rev. edn. Oxford: Clarendon Press.

Bate, Jonathan (ed.) (1992) *The Romantics on Shakespeare*. Harmondsworth: Penguin.

Bate, Jonathan (1997) *The Genius of Shakespeare*. London: Picador/Pan Macmillan.

Battenhouse, Roy (1951) 'The ghost in *Hamlet*: a catholic "linchpin"?', *Studies in Philology*, 48, 161–92.

Belsey, Catherine (1985) *The Subject of Tragedy: Identity and Difference in Renaissance Drama*. London: Methuen.

Berkoff, Steven (1989) *I am Hamlet*. London: Faber and Faber.

Berry, Ralph (1986) 'Hamlet's doubles', *Shakespeare Quarterly*, 37 (1986), 204–12.

Bevington, David (1984) *Action is Eloquence: Shakespeare's Language of Gesture*. Cambridge, MA, and London: Harvard University Press.

Bligh, John (1984) 'Shakespearian character study to 1800', *Shakespeare Survey*, 37, 141–53.

Bloom, Harold (1995) *The Western Canon: The Books and School of the Ages*. Basingstoke: Macmillan.

Bloom, Harold (1999) *Shakespeare: The Invention of the Human*. London: Fourth Estate.

Bloom, Harold (2003) *Hamlet: Poem Unlimited*. Edinburgh: Canongate Books.

Booth, Stephen (1969) 'On the value of *Hamlet*' in Rabkin, N. (ed.), *Reinterpreting Elizabethan Drama*. New York and London: Columbia University Press, 137–76.

Braden, Gordon (1985) *Renaissance Tragedy and the Senecan Tradition: Anger's Privilege*. New Haven and London: Yale University Press.

Bradley, A.C. (1992) *Shakespearean Tragedy*. 3rd edn. Basingstoke: Macmillan.

Bradley, David (1992) *From Text to Performance in the Elizabethan Theatre*. Cambridge: Cambridge University Press.

Brennan, Anthony S. (1979) 'That within which passes show: the function of the chorus in *Henry V*', *Philological Quarterly*, 58, 40–52.

Brown, John Russell and Bernard Harris (eds) (1963) *Hamlet*. Stratford-Upon-Avon Studies 5. London: Edward Arnold.

Bruster, Douglas (1992) *Drama and the Market in the Age of Shakespeare*. Cambridge: Cambridge University Press.

Bruster, Douglas (2002) 'The dramatic life of objects in the early modern theatre' in Harris and Korda (eds), *Staged Properties in Early Modern English Drama*, 67–96.

Bruster, Douglas and Robert Weimann (2004) *Prologues to Shakespeare's Theatre: Performance and Liminality in Early Modern Drama*. London and New York: Routledge/Taylor & Francis.

Burnett, Mark Thornton and John Manning (eds) (1994) *New Essays on Hamlet*. New York: AMS Press.

Burns, Edward (1990) *Character: Acting and Being on the Pre-Modern Stage*. Basingstoke, Macmillan.

Callaghan, Dympna (ed.) (2000) *A Feminist Companion to Shakespeare*. Oxford: Blackwell.

Cartmell, Deborah (2000) *Interpreting Shakespeare on Screen*. Basingstoke: Macmillan.

Cathcart, Charles (2001) '*Hamlet*: date and early afterlife', *Review of English Studies*, 52, 341–59.

Charney, Maurice (1965) '*Hamlet* without words', *English Literary History*, 32, 457–77.

Charney, Maurice (1989) 'Asides, soliloquies, and offstage speech in *Hamlet*: implications for staging' in Ruth Thompson and Jay L. Halio (eds), *Shakespeare and the Sense of Performance*. London: Associated University Presses, 116–31.

Cixous, Hélène (1974) 'The character of "character"', *New Literary History*, 5, 383–402.

Clayton, Tony (ed.) (1992) *The Hamlet First Published (Q1, 1603): Origins, Form, Intertextualities*. London and Toronto: Associated University Presses.

Conklin, Paul S. (1947) *A History of Hamlet Criticism 1601–1821*. London: Routledge & Kegan Paul.

Cox, C.B. and D.J. Palmer (eds) (1984) *Shakespeare's Wide and Universal Stage*. Manchester: Manchester University Press.

Cox, John D. and David Scott Kastan (eds) (1997) *A New History of Early English Drama*. New York: Columbia University Press.

Coyle, Martin (ed.) (1992) *Hamlet: New Casebook*. Basingstoke: Palgrave.

Cross, Brenda (ed.) (1948) *The Film Hamlet: A Record of its Production*. London: Saturn Press.

Danson, Lawrence (1983) '*Henry V*: king, chorus, and critics', *Shakespeare Quarterly*, 43, 27–43.

Davis, Philip (1996) *Sudden Shakespeare: The Shaping of Shakespeare's Creative Thought*. London: Athlone Press.

Dawson, Anthony (1995) *Shakespeare in Performance: Hamlet*. Manchester: Manchester University Press.

de Grazia, Margreta and Peter Stallybrass (1993) 'The materiality of the Shakespearean text', *Shakespeare Quarterly*, 44, 255–83.

de Grazia, Margreta, Maureen Quilligan and Peter Stallybrass (eds) (1996) *Subject and Object in Renaissance Culture*. Cambridge: Cambridge University Press.

de Grazia, Margreta (2001) '*Hamlet* before its time', *Modern Language Quarterly*, 62, 355–75.

de Grazia, Margreta (2007) *Hamlet Without Hamlet*. Cambridge: Cambridge University Press.

Desmet, Christy (1992) *Reading Shakespeare's Characters: Rhetoric, Ethics, and Identity*. Amherst, MA: University of Massachusetts Press.

Desmet, Christy (2003) 'Character criticism' in Stanley Wells and Lena Cowen Orlin (eds), *Shakespeare: An Oxford Guide*. Oxford: Oxford University Press, 351–72.

Dodd, William (1998) 'Destined livery? Character and person in Shakespeare', *Shakespeare Survey*, 51, 147–58.

Dollimore, Jonathan (2004) *Radical Tragedy: Religion, Ideology and Power in the Drama of Shakespeare and his Contemporaries*. 3rd edn. Basingstoke: Palgrave Macmillan.

Drakakis, John (ed.) (1985) *Alternative Shakespeares*. London: Methuen.

Dusinberre, Juliet (2003) *Shakespeare and the Nature of Women*. 3rd edn. London: Palgrave Macmillan.

Dutton, Richard (1989) '*Hamlet, An Apology for Actors*, and the sign of the globe', *Shakespeare Survey*, 41, 35–43.

Eagleton, Terry (1986) *William Shakespeare*. Oxford: Blackwell.

Edwards, Philip (1983) 'Tragic balance in *Hamlet*', *Shakespeare Survey*, 36, 43–52; repr. in Coyle (ed.), *Hamlet: New Casebook*, 19–36.

Eliot, T.S. (1928) 'Hamlet and his problems' in *The Sacred Wood: Essays on Poetry and Criticism*. 2nd edn. London: Methuen, 95–103.

Ellrodt, Robert (1975) 'Self-consciousness in Montaigne and Shakespeare', *Shakespeare Survey*, 28, 37–50.

Erlich, Jeremy (2002) 'The search for the *Hamlet* "director's cut" ', *English Studies*, 83, 399–406.

Evans, Robert C. (1999) 'Friendship in *Hamlet*', *Comparative Drama*, 33, 88–124.

Foakes, R.A. (1954) 'The player's passion: some notes on Elizabethan psychology and acting', *Essays and Studies*, 7, 62–77.

Foakes, R.A. (1956) '*Hamlet* and the court of Elsinore', *Shakespeare Survey*, 9, 35–43.

Foakes, R.A. (1963) 'Character and speech in *Hamlet*' in Brown and Harris (eds), *Hamlet*, 148–62.

Foakes, R.A. (1993) *Hamlet Versus Lear: Cultural Politics and Shakespeare's Art*. Cambridge: Cambridge University Press.

Foakes, R.A. (2005) ' "Armed at point exactly": the ghost in *Hamlet*', *Shakespeare Survey*, 58, 34–47.

Forker, Charles R. (1963) 'Shakespeare's theatrical symbolism and its function', *Shakespeare Quarterly*, 14, 215–29.

Freeman, John (2003) 'This side of purgatory: ghostly fathers and the recusant legacy in *Hamlet*' in Taylor and Beauregard (eds), *Shakespeare and the Culture of Christianity in Early Modern England*, 222–59.

Freud, Sigmund (1976) *The Interpretation of Dreams*. Trans. James Strachey. Harmondsworth: Penguin.

Frye, Roland Mushat (1984) *The Renaissance Hamlet: Issues and Responses in 1600*. Princeton, NJ: Princeton University Press.

Goldberg, Jonathan (1986) 'Textual properties', *Shakespeare Quarterly*, 37, 213–17.

Goldberg, Jonathan (1988) 'Hamlet's hand', *Shakespeare Quarterly*, 39, 307–27.

Goldman, Michael (1985) *Acting and Action in Shakespearean Tragedy*. Princeton, NJ: Princeton University Press.

Grady, Hugh (2002) *Shakespeare, Machiavelli, and Montaigne: Power and Subjectivity From Richard II to Hamlet*. Oxford: Oxford University Press.

Greenblatt, Stephen (1980) *Renaissance Self-Fashioning: From More to Shakespeare*. Chicago and London: University of Chicago Press.

Greenblatt, Stephen (1988) *Shakespearean Negotiations: The Circulation of Social Energy in Renaissance England*. Oxford: Clarendon Press.

Greenblatt, Stephen (2001) *Hamlet in Purgatory*. Princeton, NJ: Princeton University Press.

Gurr, Andrew (1992) *The Shakespearean Stage 1574–1642*. 3rd edn. Cambridge: Cambridge University Press

Gurr, Andrew and Mariko Ichikawa (2000) *Staging in Shakespeare's Theatres*. Oxford: Oxford University Press.

Hall, Donald E., (2004) *Subjectivity*. London and New York: Routledge/Taylor & Francis.

Hardin, Craig (1964) 'Hamlet as a man of action', *Huntington Library Quarterly*, 27, 229–37.

Harris, Jonathan Gil and Korda, Natasha (eds) (2002) *Staged Properties in Early Modern English Drama*. Cambridge: Cambridge University Press.

Harvey, John (1995) *Men in Black*. London: Reaktion Books.

Hassel, R. Chris, Jr. (2003) 'The accent and gait of Christians: Hamlet's puritan style' in Taylor and Beauregard (eds), *Shakespeare and the Culture of Christianity in Early Modern England*, 287–310.

Hawkes, Terence (1973) *Shakespeare's Talking Animals: Language and Drama in Society*. London: Edward Arnold.

Hawkes, Terence (1985) '*Telmah*' in Parker and Hartman (eds), *Shakespeare and the Question of Theory*, 310–32.

Hawkes, Terence (ed.) (1996) *Alternative Shakespeares: Volume 2*. London: Routledge.

Heilbrun, Carolyn (1957) 'The character of Hamlet's mother', *Shakespeare Quarterly*, 8, 201–26.

Hillman, Richard (1997) *Self-Speaking in Medieval and Early Modern English Drama: Subjectivity, Discourse and the Stage*. Basingstoke, Macmillan.

Hirsh, James (1997) 'Shakespeare and the history of soliloquies', *Modern Language Quarterly*, 58, 1–26.

Holmes, Jonathan (2004) *Merely Players? Actors Accounts of Performing Shakespeare*. London and New York: Routledge/Taylor & Francis.

Honigmann, E.A.J. (1956) 'The date of *Hamlet*', *Shakespeare Survey*, 9, 24–34.

Honigmann, E.A.J. (1963) 'The politics in *Hamlet* and "the world of the play" in Brown and Harris (eds), *Hamlet*, 129–47.

Horwich, Richard (1971) '*Hamlet* and *Eastward Ho*', *Studies in English Literature*, 11, 223–33.

Hunter, G.K. (1980) '"Flatcaps and bluecoats": visual signs on the Elizabethan stage', *Essays and Studies*, 30, 16–47.

Hussey, S.S. (1992) *The Literary Language of Shakespeare*. 2nd edn. London and New York: Longman.

Hutson, Lorna (2002) 'From penitent to suspect: law, purgatory, and renaissance drama', *Huntington Library Quarterly*, 65, 295–319.

Hutson, Lorna (2005) 'Rethinking the "spectacle of the scaffold": juridical epistemologies and English revenge tragedy', *Representations*, 89, 30–58.

Jackson, Russell (2000) (ed.) *The Cambridge Companion to Shakespeare on Film*. Cambridge: Cambridge University Press.

Jardine, Lisa (1983) *Still Harping on Daughters: Women and Drama in the Age of Shakespeare*. Brighton: New Harvester.

Jardine, Lisa (1996) *Reading Shakespeare Historically*. London and New York: Routledge.

Johnson, Samuel (1989) *Samuel Johnson on Shakespeare*. Ed. W.R. Woodhuysen. Harmondsworth: Penguin.

Jones, Ann Rosalind and Peter Stallybrass (2000) *Renaissance Clothing and the Materials of Memory*. Cambridge: Cambridge University Press.

Jones, Ernest (1949) *Hamlet and Oedipus*. London: Victor Gollancz.

Jones, John (1995) *Shakespeare at Work*. Oxford: Clarendon Press.

Joseph, Miriam (1961) 'Discerning the ghost in *Hamlet*', *PMLA: Publications of the Modern Language Association of America*, 76, 493–502.

Jump, John (ed.) (1968) *Hamlet: A Casebook*. London: Macmillan.

Kastan, David Scott and Peter Stallybrass (eds) (1991) *Staging the Renaissance: Reinterpretations of Elizabethan and Jacobean Drama*. New York and London: Routledge.

Kastan, David Scott (1999) *Shakespeare After Theory*. London: Routledge.

Kastan, David Scott (2001) *Shakespeare and the Book*. Cambridge: Cambridge University Press.

Kehler, Dorothea (1995) 'The first quarto of *Hamlet*: reforming widow Gertred', *Shakespeare Quarterly*, 46, 398–413.

Kerrigan, John (1981) 'Hieronimo, Hamlet, and remembrance', *Essays in Criticism*, 31, 105–26.

Kerrigan, John (1996) *Revenge Tragedy: Aeschylus to Armageddon*. Oxford: Clarendon Press.

Kerrigan, William (1994) *Hamlet's Perfection*. Baltimore, Maryland and London: Johns Hopkins University Press.

Kinney, Arthur (ed.) (2002) *Hamlet: New Critical Essays*. London and New York: Routledge.

Kliman, Bernice W. (1988) *Hamlet: Film, Television, and Audio Performance*. London and Toronto: Associated University Presses.

Knight, G. Wilson (1949) *The Wheel of Fire: Interpretations of Shakespearian Tragedy*. Rev. edn. London: Methuen.

Knights, L.C. (1946) 'How many children had Lady Macbeth?' in *Explorations*. London: Chatto & Windus, 1–39.

Knights, L.C. (1965) 'The question of character in Shakespeare', in *Further Explorations*. London: Chatto & Windus, 186–204.

Knights, L.C. (1966) *Some Shakespearean Themes and An Approach to Hamlet*. Harmondsworth: Penguin.

Kott, Jan (1965) *Shakespeare Our Contemporary*. Trans. Boleslaw Taborski. Preface by Peter Brook. London: Methuen.

Lacan, Jacques (1977) 'Desire and the interpretation of desire in *Hamlet*', ed. Jacques-Alain Miller and trans. James Hulbert. *Yale French Studies*, 55/56, 11–52.

Lanham, Richard A. (1976) *The Motives of Eloquence: Literary Rhetoric in the Renaissance*. New Haven and London: Yale University Press.

Lanham, Richard A. (1991) *A Handlist of Rhetorical Terms*. 2nd edn. Berkeley, Los Angeles, CA., and London: University of California Press.

Lee, John (2000) *Shakespeare's Hamlet and the Controversies of Self*. Oxford: Clarendon Press.

Levin, Harry (1959) *The Question of Hamlet*. New York: Oxford University Press.

Lewis, C.S. (1969) 'Hamlet: the prince or the poem?' in *Selected Literary Essays*. Cambridge: Cambridge University Press, 88–105.

Loewenstein, Joseph (1988) 'Plays agonistic and competitive: the textual approach to Elsinore', *Renaissance Drama*, 19, 63–96.

Low, Anthony (1999) '*Hamlet* and the ghost of purgatory: intimations of killing the father', *English Literary Renaissance*, 29, 443–67.

Lyons, Bridget Gellert (1971) *Voices of Melancholy: Studies in Literary Treatments of Melancholy in Renaissance England*. London: Routledge & Kegan Paul.

Lyons, Bridget Gellert (1977) 'The iconography of Ophelia', *English Literary History*, 44, 60–74.

Marcus, Leah S. (1996) *Unediting the Renaissance: Shakespeare, Marlowe, Milton*. London and New York: Routledge.

Matheson, Mark (1995) 'Hamlet and a "matter tender and dangerous"', *Shakespeare Quarterly*, 46, 383–97.

Maxwell, Baldwin (1964) 'Hamlet's mother', *Shakespeare Quarterly*, 15, 235–46.

MacFaul, Thomas (2007) *Male Friendship in Shakespeare and his Contemporaries*. Cambridge: Cambridge University Press.

Maus, Katharine Eisaman (1995) *Inwardness and Theater in the English Renaissance*. Chicago: University of Chicago Press.

McAlindon, T. (1973) *Shakespeare and Decorum*. London and Basingstoke: Macmillan.

McCabe, Richard A. (1993) *Incest, Drama and Nature's Law 1550–1700*. Cambridge: Cambridge University Press.

McDonald, Russ (1988) *Shakespeare and Jonson, Jonson and Shakespeare*. Lincoln, Nebraska, and London: University of Nebraska Press.

McLoud, Randall [published under Random Cloud] (1982) 'The marriage of good and bad quartos', *Shakespeare Quarterly*, 33, 421–31.

McLoud, Randall [published under Random Cloud] (1991) ' "The very names of the persons": editing and the invention of dramatick character' in Kastan and Stallybrass (eds), *Staging the Renaissance*, 88–96.

McEvoy, Sean (ed.) (2006) *Hamlet: A Sourcebook*. London and New York: Routledge/Taylor & Francis.

McGee, Arthur (1987) *The Elizabethan Hamlet*. New Haven and London: Yale University Press.

Mercer, Peter (1987) *Hamlet and the Acting of Revenge*. Basingstoke, Macmillan.

Mills, John A. (1985) *Hamlet on Stage: The Great Tradition*. London: Greenwood Press.

Miola, Robert S. (2000) *Shakespeare's Reading*. Oxford: Oxford University Press.

Moorman, F. W. (1906) 'Shakespeare's ghosts', *Modern Language Review*, 1, 192–201.

Mowat, Barbara A. (1983) ' "The getting up of the spectacle": the role of the visual on the Elizabethan stage, 1576–1600', *The Elizabethan Theatre*, 9, 60–76.

Mowat, Barbara (1988) 'The form of *Hamlet*'s fortunes', *Renaissance Drama*, 19, 97–126.

Muir, Kenneth (1977) 'The singularity of Shakespeare', in *The Singularity of Shakespeare and Other Essays*. Liverpool: Liverpool University Press, 124–37.

Muir, Kenneth (1977) *The Sources of Shakespeare's Plays*. London: Methuen.

Muir, Kenneth (1981) 'Shakespeare's open secret', *Shakespeare Survey*, 34, 1–9.

Murphy, Andrew (ed.) (2000) *The Renaissance Text: Theory, Editing, Textuality*. Manchester: Manchester University Press.

Newell, Alex (1991) *The Soliloquies in Hamlet: The Structural Design*. London: Associated University Presses.

Nuttall, A.D. (1984) 'The argument about Shakespeare's characters' in Cox and Palmer (eds), *Shakespeare's Wide and Universal Stage*, 18–31.

Nuttall, A.D. (2007) *A New Mimesis: Shakespeare and the Representation of Reality*. 2nd edn. New Haven and London: Yale University Press.

O'Brian, Ellen J. (1992) 'Revision by excision: rewriting Gertrude', *Shakespeare Survey*, 45, 27–35.

Orgel, Stephen (1988) 'The authentic Shakespeare', *Representations*, 21, 1–25.

Orgel, Stephen (2002) *The Authentic Shakespeare and Other Problems of the Early Modern Stage*. London and New York: Routledge.

Ouditt, Sharon (1996), 'Explaining woman's frailty: feminist readings of Gertrude', in Smith and Wood (eds), *Hamlet: Theory in Practice*, 83–107.

Palfrey, Simon (2005) *Doing Shakespeare*. London: Arden Shakespeare/Thomson Learning.

Palmer, D.J. (1982) ' "We shall know by this fellow": prologue and chorus in Shakespeare', *Bulletin of the John Rylands University Library of Manchester*, 64, 501–21.

Paris, Bernard J. (1991) *Character as a Subversive Force in Shakespeare*. London and Toronto: Associated University Presses.

Parker, G.F. (1989) *Johnson's Shakespeare*. Oxford: Clarendon Press.

Parker, Patricia and Geoffrey Hartman (eds) (1985) *Shakespeare and the Question of Theory*. London and New York: Methuen.

Pennington, Michael (1996) *Hamlet: A User's Guide*. London: Nick Hern Books.

Pirie, David (1984) '*Hamlet* without the prince' in Cox and Palmer (eds), *Shakespeare's Wide and Universal Stage*, 164–84.

Prosser, Eleanor (1967) *Hamlet and Revenge*. Stanford: Stanford University Press.

Ronk, Martha C. (1994) 'Representations of Ophelia', *Criticism*, 36, 21–43.

Rose, Jacqueline (1985) 'Sexuality in the reading of Shakespeare: *Hamlet* and *Measure for Measure*', in Drakakis (ed.), *Alternative Shakespeares*, 95–118.

Rosenblatt, Jason P. (1978) 'Aspects of the incest problem in *Hamlet*', *Shakespeare Quarterly*, 29, 349–64.

Rothwell, Kenneth S. (2004) *A History of Shakespeare on Screen: A Century of Film and Television*. 2nd edn. Cambridge: Cambridge University Press.

Rust, Jennifer (2003) 'Wittenberg and melancholic allegory: the reformation and its discontents in *Hamlet*' in Taylor and Beauregard (eds), *Shakespeare and the Culture of Christianity in Early Modern England*, 260–86.

Shapiro, James (2005) *1599: A Year in the Life of William Shakespeare*. London: Faber and Faber.

Showalter, Elaine (1985) 'Representing Ophelia: women, madness, and the responsibilities of feminist criticism' in Parker and Hartman (eds), *Shakespeare and the Question of Theory*, 77–94.

Siegel, Paul N. (1992) ' "Hamlet, revenge!": the uses and abuses of historical criticism', *Shakespeare Survey*, 45, 15–26.

Sinfield, Alan (1980) 'Hamlet's special providence', *Shakespeare Survey*, 33, 89–97.

Sinfield, Alan (1992) *Faultlines: Cultural Materialism and the Politics of Dissident Reading*. Oxford: Clarendon Press.

Smith, Emma (2000) 'Ghost writing: *Hamlet* and the *Ur-Hamlet*' in A. Murphy (ed.), *The Renaissance Text*, 177–90.

Smith, Peter J. and Nigel Wood (eds) (1996) *Hamlet: Theory in Practice*. Buckingham and Philadelphia: Open University Press.

Smith, Rebecca (1992) 'A heart cleft in twain: the dilemma of Shakespeare's Gertrude', in Coyle (ed.), *Hamlet: New Casebook*, 80–95.

Sofer, Andrew (1998) 'The skull on the renaissance stage', *English Literary Renaissance*, 28, 47–77.

Sofer, Andrew (2003) *The Stage Life of Props*. Ann Arbor: University of Michigan Press.

Stallybrass, Peter (2000) 'Naming, renaming, and unnaming in the Shakespearean quartos and folios' in A. Murphy (ed.), *The Renaissance Text*,108–34.

States, Bert O. (1992) *Hamlet and the Concept of Character*. Baltimore and London: Johns Hopkins University Press.

Stern, Tiffany (2004) *Making Shakespeare: From Stage to Page*. London and New York: Routledge.

Taylor, Dennis and David N. Beauregard (eds) (2003) *Shakespeare and the Culture of Christianity in Early Modern England*. New York: Fordham University Press.

Taylor, Neil (1994) 'The films of *Hamlet*' in Anthony Davies and Stanley Wells (eds), *Shakespeare and the Moving Image: The Plays on Film and Television*, 180–95.

Thompson, Ann (2003) 'Infinite jest: the comedy of *Hamlet, Prince of Denmark*', *Shakespeare Survey*, 56, 93–104.

Thomson, Peter (1992) *Shakespeare's Theatre*. 2nd edn. London: Routledge.

Thomson, Peter (1997) 'Rogues and rhetoricians: acting styles in early English drama' in Cox and Kastan (eds), *A New History of Early English Drama*, 321–35.

Ure, Peter (1963) 'Character and role from Richard III to Hamlet' in Brown and Harris (eds), *Hamlet*, 148–62.

Urkowitz, Steven (1986) ' "Well-sayd olde mole": burying three *Hamlets* in modern editions' in G. Ziegler (ed.), *Shakespeare Study Today*. New York: AMS Press, 37–70.

Vickers, Brian (ed.) (1974–81) *Shakespeare: The Critical Heritage*. 6 vols. London: Routledge & Kegan Paul.

Vickers, Brian (1981) 'The emergence of character criticism, 1774–1800', *Shakespeare Survey*, 34, 11–21.

Waddington, Raymond (1989) 'Lutheran Hamlet', *English Language Notes*, 25, 27–42.

Walsh, Marcus (1997) *Shakespeare, Milton, and Eighteenth-Century Literary Editing*. Cambridge: Cambridge University Press.

Ward, David (1992) 'The king and *Hamlet*', *Shakespeare Quarterly*, 43, 280–302.

Watson, Robert N. (1990) 'Giving up the ghost in a world of decay: Hamlet, revenge, and denial', *Renaissance Drama*, 21, 199–223.

Weil, Herbert S., Jr (1981) 'On expectation and surprise: Shakespeare's construction of character', *Shakespeare Survey*, 34, 39–50.

Weimann, Robert (1981) 'Society and the individual in Shakespeare's conception of character', *Shakespeare Survey*, 34, 23–31.

Weimann, Robert (2000) *Author's Pen and Actor's Voice: Playing and Writing in Shakespeare's Theatre*. Cambridge: Cambridge University Press.

Wells, Robin Headlam (2000) *Shakespeare on Masculinity*. Cambridge: Cambridge University Press.

Wells, Stanley (ed.) (1990) *Shakespeare: A Bibliographical Guide*. New Edition. Oxford: Oxford University Press.

Wells, Stanley (ed.) (1997) *Shakespeare in the Theatre: An Anthology of Criticism*. Oxford: Oxford University Press.

Werstine, Paul (1988) 'The textual mystery of *Hamlet*', *Shakespeare Quarterly*, 39, 1–26.

Werstine, Paul (1990) 'Narratives about printed Shakespeare texts: "foul papers" and "bad" quartos', *Shakespeare Quarterly*, 41, 65–86.

West, Robert H. (1955) 'King Hamlet's ambiguous ghost', *PMLA: Publications of the Modern Language Association of America*, 70, 1107–17.

Wheale, Nigel (1996) ' "Vnfolde your selfe": Jacques Lacan and the psychoanalytic reading of *Hamlet*' in Smith and Wood (eds), *Hamlet: Theory in Practice*, 108–32.

Williamson, Claude C.H. (1950) *Readings on the Character of Hamlet, 1661–1947*. London: Allen & Unwin.

Wilson, John Dover (1951) *What Happens in Hamlet*. 3rd edn. Cambridge: Cambridge University Press.

Wright, George T. (1981) 'Hendiadys and *Hamlet*', *PMLA: Publications of the Modern Language Association of America*, 96, 168–93.

SELECTED FILMS OF *HAMLET*

Hamlet (1948) Dir. Laurence Olivier. UK. Two Cities Films.
Hamlet (1964) Dir. Grigori Kozintzev. USSR. LenFilm.
Hamlet (1969) Dir. Tony Richardson. UK. Woodfall.
Hamlet (1990) Dir. Franco Zeffirelli. USA. Carolco.
Hamlet (2000) Dir. Michael Almereyda. USA. Miramax.

INDEX